P9-DHA-323

Poverty
Is a Personal Thing!

"Poverty is taking your children to the hospital and spending the whole day waiting with no one even taking your name, and then coming back the next, and the next, until they finally get around to you.

"Poverty is having a landlady who is a public health nurse who turns off the heat when she leaves for work....

"Poverty is having a child with glaucoma and watching that eye condition grow worse every day, while the welfare officials send you to the private agencies, and the private agencies send you back to the welfare...."

Statement by Mrs. Janice Bradshaw,
quoted by Sargent Shriver

Here are the firsthand experiences of the poor, the raw facts of life for one-fifth of our nation, with articles by John Kenneth Galbraith, Michael Harrington, Walter Reuther, Franklin Delano Roosevelt, Caroline Bird, and Martin Luther King, Jr.

PROBLEMS OF AMERICAN SOCIETY

Focusing on the urban scene, youth, the individual and his search for a better life, the books in this series probe the most crucial dilemmas of our time.

Air and Water Pollution
The City As a Community
*City Government
Civil Rights and Civil Liberties
The Consumer
Crime and Juvenile Delinquency
The Draft
Drugs
*Hunger
The Negro in the City
*Minorities All
Poverty and the Poor
*Racism
Riots
Slums
The Traffic Jam

* Forthcoming

HC110
P6
L39

GERALD LEINWAND

assisted by
Elsie Collins

Poverty
and
the Poor

WSP
Ⓝ WASHINGTON SQUARE PRESS   NEW YORK

JAN 13 '72

165527

POVERTY AND THE POOR

A *Washington Square Press* edition
1st printing.....................December, 1968

Published by Washington Square Press,
a division of Simon & Schuster, Inc., 630 Fifth Avenue, New York, N.Y.

WASHINGTON SQUARE PRESS editions are distributed in the
U.S. by Simon & Schuster, Inc., 630 Fifth Avenue, New
York, N.Y. 10020 and in Canada by Simon & Schuster
of Canada, Ltd., Richmond Hill, Ontario, Canada.

Standard Book Number: 671-47857-7.
Copyright, ©, 1968, by Simon & Schuster, Inc. All rights reserved.
Printed in the U.S.A.

*To my parents
who taught me to live
in urban America*

Preface

While it is difficult to generalize about the problems of poverty, a number of things are clear. For one thing, while poverty has long been the common experience of man, in a rich society poverty is the leading contradiction of our time. For another, far from being uplifting, as some have thought, poverty is degrading and is a harsh and cruel experience for those who are caught in its grip. It is also clear that we have within our society the means by which the side-effects of poverty may be at least partially reduced, even if poverty itself is not likely to be totally eliminated in the foreseeable future.

This book represents an effort to make the problem of urban poverty understandable to today's students. It tries to identify the changing attitudes toward poverty in American society and to suggest how those attitudes came to be changed. The problems with which this book deals are complex and controversial. We have tried to make them understandable. We have also tried to present the problem realistically so that the reader, whatever his own financial situation, can acquire a better insight into the nature of the problem and perhaps be in a better position to take appropriate action to end poverty.

Preface

One of the difficulties in dealing with poverty is that it is very hard to know how many poor there are at any time. Much depends on income, the cost of living, and where the people live. The figures in this volume are approximate only.

As do other volumes in this series, this book begins with a brief overview of the problems of urban poverty. Following the essay are fifteen selected, annotated readings designed to identify various facets of the problem of poverty. The essay and the readings that follow will not provide answers. They raise questions, create doubts, and encourage further reading and inquiry into the problem. This is an introductory study only and can be but a beginning in the examination of a complex problem. But, as an old Chinese proverb declares, "A journey of a thousand miles begins by taking a single step." We hope that the study of the problem of poverty will be at least the first step along a difficult journey in the course of which some contribution may be made to a solution of the problems of urban poverty.

G. L.

Contents

Contents

Part One

The Problem
and the Challenge

THE job-seekers who shuffle along the dingy halls of lower Manhattan employment centers are looking for jobs requiring few, if any, skills. They are pitiful to look at. They wear ill-fitting clothes and dirty shirts that were probably once white. Judged by standards of other countries, these people are not poor. But by America's standards these people are very poor indeed. The poor in America number about 25 million. These Americans exist in conditions of want or near want. While they make up about 20 percent of the population, these people live in what has been called an "invisible land."[1] While poverty is rural as well as urban in nature, the cities of America have become "the frontiers of the poor."[2] It is to make the urban poor more visible that this book is devoted. It will try to explain what poverty is, where the poor are, who the poor are, how they came to be poor, why they stay poor, and some of the things that are being tried to help them.

What Is Poverty?

To be poor means not having enough money to live decently. Some people have always been poor. Indeed, throughout the history of the world most

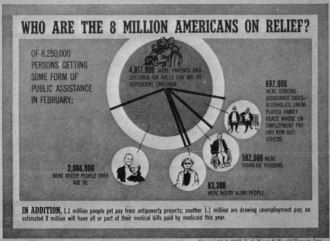

WHO ARE THE 8 MILLION AMERICANS ON RELIEF?

OF 8,250,000 PERSONS GETTING SOME FORM OF PUBLIC ASSISTANCE IN FEBRUARY:

4,817,000 WERE PARENTS AND CHILDREN ON ROLLS FOR AID TO DEPENDENT CHILDREN.

692,000 WERE GENERAL-ASSISTANCE CASES—ALCOHOLICS; UNEMPLOYED FAMILY HEADS WHOSE UNEMPLOYMENT PAY HAD RUN OUT; OTHERS.

2,066,000 WERE NEEDY PEOPLE OVER AGE 65.

592,000 WERE DISABLED PERSONS.

83,300 WERE NEEDY BLIND PEOPLE.

IN ADDITION, 1.1 million people get pay from antipoverty projects; another 1.1 million are drawing unemployment pay; an estimated 8 million will have all or part of their medical bills paid by medicaid this year.

Copyright © 1967, U. S. News & World Report, Inc.

people were born poor and stayed poor the rest of their lives. In America the great majority of the people is not poor. If about 80 percent can live in relative comfort, why does such comfort appear almost beyond the reach of the remaining 20 percent? The continued existence of poverty in the midst of riches has been called the "paradox of poverty." A paradox is a riddle or a puzzle which seems to have no explanation. Why some people remain in want, while most have what they need, is one part of the puzzle of poverty. Another is that poverty is difficult to define. According to Sargent Shriver, former head of the United States Office of Economic Opportunity, "Anybody is poor who has less than 23 cents a meal, a day, plus $1.40 for everything else."[3] But these figures do not tell the whole story of what poverty is. Some people are poor who have higher incomes. There may be special circumstances, such as large families, unusual illness, or the need to care for aged parents, which contribute to poverty. Much also depends on what a given amount of money will buy at any given time.

Whatever the precise dollar figure of poverty may be, in a real sense "only the poor can know poverty; only they can understand it."[4] Neither the social worker who tries to help, nor the newspaper reporter who tries to find out, nor the economist who tries to define poverty can really know it. To be poor is to wear cheap clothes. The fact that these cheap clothes may, at a glance, look like the clothes of the rich is one of the factors which help to make poverty invisible. The poor live in miserable homes in run-down neighborhoods where the prosperous American rarely goes. To be poor is to buy food of poor quality and to eat an unbalanced diet which contributes to ill health. To be poor is to learn to accept handouts, and to accept poverty as a way of life.

If one can read the faces of the poor, one can understand the meaning of poverty. The dirty streets, the run-down homes, the crowded apartments, yelling children, the limited play areas, the stench of garbage, are all part of the meaning of poverty. Poverty robs the individual of his dignity. He cannot live as the well-to-do American lives because he is caught in a vise of poverty. From this vise he is unable to escape. Yet his desires, needs, and longings are just as real as those of any other American. But for 20 percent of the population these needs and longings are unlikely to be fulfilled during the course of their lifetime. To make matters worse, children of the poor can expect to be poor themselves. Soon a culture of poverty* develops which seems to have its own reason for

---

culture of poverty—term first used by Oscar Lewis.

(OEO)

16

(OEO)

being. It feeds upon itself and drags the poor down and, along with them, their children—and even their children's children.

> Every magazine and TV advertisement, with its beautiful women and sleek cars and new washing machines, shouts at them that they are failures, for they do not share in your picture of what American life is like.[5]

Poverty makes it impossible for the poor to share in the picture of what the American way of life is supposed to be.

Writing in 1904, Robert Hunter was one of the first men to recognize poverty as a special condition. He defined poverty as a family of four having an income of less than about $460 per year.[6] If today we define poverty as less than $3,300 a year, it would appear that we are much better off than we were before. But such is not the case. In the years when Hunter wrote, the prices people paid for things they needed were much lower. Even more important, however, in those days it was expected that many would indeed be poor. Hunter's contribution to the problem of poverty was that he was among the first to recognize that we could, and should, do something about it. In 1904 we could, perhaps, expect a great many people to be living at or near poverty levels; but today, with our greater abundance, it is shameful that anyone should live at a level that can be described as poor or deprived.

Who Are the Poor?

> Rosita P., age 47, cooks at the stove of her tiny kitchen (three feet by five feet) on New York City's Lower East Side. She had come to New York 12 years before. Rosita lives entirely on her welfare

Shown with one of her ten children this resident of Chicago's West Side ghetto asks, "What did I do to my family not to be able to help them?" (Wide World)

check; her husband disappeared years ago. To support herself and her two children, she receives $99 every two weeks. Of this nearly half . . . goes to the landlord as rent for their ill-lighted, over-heated three-room flat in the basement of a dilapidated apartment building. With the rest, she buys food, second hand clothing, an occasional item of furniture. An old TV set and an equally aged record player provide entertainment.[7]

She is one of the invisible Americans—the poor among us. The poor are those who have been without jobs for a long time and those who get jobs only occasionally. The poor are those whose incomes do not meet their reasonable needs. Often the poor are physically or mentally sick and, as a result, are unable to work. Included among the poor are men and women whose skills have been replaced by a machine. Among the poor are those who are too old to work and who have used up whatever savings they may have had. Among the poor are old people who have earned a pension during their youth but now find that these payments, made for past services, are not big enough to pay for today's or tomorrow's needs. The poor are ill-educated young people who have dropped out of school. Minority groups—Negroes, Puerto Ricans, Mexicans—suffer particularly.

The poor in the United States may be said to have a number of things in common. Indeed, one writer has described this "formula" for being poor. A person runs the risk of becoming poor if several of the following appy to him:

1. He is non-white.
2. He belongs to a family with no earners.
3. He belongs to a family whose head is female.
4. He belongs to a family with more than six children under 18.
5. He is between 14 and 25 or over 65.
6. He lives in a rural farm area.
7. He has fewer than eight years of education.
8. He lives in the South.[8]

This so-called formula tells us something about poverty. It tells us that a person who is non-white is more likely to be poor than a white person. Indeed, in the slums of northern cities the bulk of the poor are Negroes. However, it is well to understand that when the poor are counted in the nation as a whole, more whites than Negroes are poor. The important thing, however, is that poor Negroes make up a larger proportion of the Negro population of the United States than is the case for poor whites. While only 10 percent of the

America's unemployed citizens gather on the city streets, knowing that they will probably do the same thing tomorrow and the next day (OEO)

white people are poor, about 20 percent of the Negroes are poor. This formula tells us something else. It tells us that those who live on farms or in rural areas run a greater risk of being poor than do those who live in cities. While this book is chiefly about the appalling effects of urban poverty, it is well to keep in mind that poverty in rural areas is probably deeper and more resistant to some reasonable solution than is poverty in urban areas. This formula also shows very clearly the relationship between education and poverty. Those with little education, those who have not learned skills useful in industry, are among the candidates for poverty. The unemployed youth and those over 65 who cannot work make up a large portion of the poor. Families that are excessively large, living on resources that are too limited to support them, are among those who may be called poor.

It was the noted Harvard economist John Kenneth Galbraith who, in his book *The Affluent Society,*[9] called our attention to the riddle of poverty in a rich society. He described poverty as being of two main kinds. The first, *case poverty,* is the kind that grows out of some characteristic that an individual or family has—ill health, not enough education, or addiction to alcohol or narcotics. The second, *insular poverty,* is the kind that exists in a community where "everybody," or nearly everybody, is poor. The Appalachia region in West Virginia is an example. Those who live in the slum ghettos of large cities may also be said to be living on an island of poverty in an ocean of wealth. There is no easy cure for either kind of poverty. A person who is poor because of some circumstance peculiar to the kind of life he lives may try to do something about it. But those who are poor because they are ill cannot really do very much to regain health, get a job, earn an income, and provide themselves with an adequate minimum standard of comfort. In these islands of poverty, both in rural areas and in urban slums, it is difficult—if not impossible—for a person to pull himself out through his own efforts.

Where Do the Poor Live?

Although it has been said that the poor are "invisible," in a geographic sense the poor are everywhere. They are in the city and in the country. They are in the North as well as the South. During the last ten years, the proportion of poor families to the total population in the major geographic regions of the United States—the South, the Northeast, the North Central states, and the West—has changed very little, if at all. About 15 percent of poor families live on farms. About 25 percent live in the slums of central cities.[10] The rest live in rural non-farm areas and in the suburbs of large cities. While the suburbs are ordinarily thought of as being made up of the relatively prosperous, it may come as a surprise to realize that there are any poor people in suburbia at all. Yet they exist and their problems are very real.

Probably the two best-known geographic pockets of poverty are in Appalachia and in the Upper Great Lakes states. Appalachia is the name given to the area which cuts across ten states from northern Pennsylvania to northern Alabama. It is about ten times the size of Switzerland. The Upper Great Lakes region is located in the northern reaches of Michigan, Minnesota, and Wisconsin. In both areas may be found examples of urban and rural poverty. The poverty of these regions has deep roots and a long history. Mainly it grows out of the wasteful use of natural resources upon which the prosperity of the people living in these areas depends. In Appalachia coal mining was the chief oc-

A West Virginia father of seven, left jobless when the strip-mines closed down, carries water to his dilapidated hill home (OEO)

cupation of the people. Instead of the coal and other minerals of the area being used wisely, they were removed wastefully in an effort to "get rich quick." Instead of the realization that minerals, once used up, would not quickly be replaced, there was little thought given as to what might be done in the future to save the prosperity of the region. Appalachia once had fine soil and tall trees, but the tall trees were recklessly cut down and the fine soil was misused through unwise methods of farming. When machines began to replace men in the mines and on the farms, the situation became worse. The combination of forces—wasteful use of mines and farms, the replacement of men by machines, inadequate funds for schools and hospitals—all led to the state of poverty. Whether you compare rural areas in Appalachia with rural areas elsewhere, urban areas with cities elsewhere, the rural and urban areas of this region lag far behind the rest of America.[11]

In the Upper Great Lakes area, forces similar to those in Appalachia were at work to bring poverty to a once rich region. The resources of the region were timber and rich iron ore. While both formed a basis upon which the prosperity of the area could be built, both were quickly utilized with little thought given as to what would replace them when they were no longer available. Today the iron ores are not as high in quality as they once were. This makes the ores less desirable than those elsewhere. The ores do not bring as high a price, as buyers prefer higher quality iron ore. Because iron ore seemed so available, there was little thought given to other industries that could have been developed. Moreover, the use of new processes has contributed to unemployment with the result that unemployment in this area is about twice as high as it is in the nation generally. As a result of a combination of these forces—wasteful use of old resources and failure to develop new industries—this area, too, in its cities and on its farms, began to feel the full meaning of poverty.

Poverty in the future will be largely urban poverty. This is true, if for no other reason than the fact that the cities are growing. It is to the central city that those from minority groups, mainly Negroes and Puerto Ricans, have been coming. "The poor now live predominantly in the central city areas left behind by the once poor."[12] It is in the city and among those already poor that poverty is likely to linger and to resist such progress and improvement that may be made.

What Has Been Our Past Attitude toward the Poor?

It is only since the late nineteenth century or so that there has been any real concern on the part of government for the poor. In general, it was felt that the poor deserved their fate. By being poor they were only paying a fair price for their sins. These sins were believed to be laziness, lack of ambition, indifference, wasteful habits of living, idleness, and extravagance. While this attitude was true of Europe as well as America, it was in America that the myth of the self-made man was born. For generations it was believed that any boy with ambition could rise from rags to riches if only he had the drive and did the hard work such a rise required. In general the idea prevailed that those who were poor had simply been unable to survive the battle in the natural struggle among men for wealth, power, and position. That the strong should survive and prosper and that the weak should remain poor was regarded as natural and just.

Contributing to this attitude toward the poor was the idea that in the commercial life of a nation it was best to leave business alone. The laws of the market place, so it was thought, would make prices of goods and wages for labor fair at most times. The general feeling was that when business was poor, unemployment high, wages low, it was only a matter of time before things would right themselves. Wages would rise, jobs would grow and business would prosper, all without the intervention of the government.

During most of the nineteenth century, men and governments were slow to recognize what poverty really was. Instead, they insisted that poverty was good for the soul, that it had a purifying effect on man. They said that wealth only corrupted the simple but wholesome lives of the poor. Poverty was needed to strengthen character and to toughen the moral fiber of man. Andrew Carnegie, a famous American industrialist, wrote, "The greatest and best of our race have necessarily been nurtured in the bracing school of poverty—the only school capable of producing the supremely great."[13]

Child labor was common among the poor at the turn of the century. It was believed that an ambitious boy could rise by his own efforts, as indeed many did (Lewis Hines Collection, New York Public Library)

How Have We Tried to Help the Poor in the Past?

The kind of assistance the poor were given depended in large measure on the attitude toward the poor at the time. Since the attitude until quite recently was, as we have seen, that with few exceptions the poor deserved their fate, the main emphasis was not so much on their poverty as on their morals. The object of public and private charity was to make the poor industrious and sober, careful and thrifty. Churches insisted that the way out of poverty was piety and that the road to prosperity was prayer. There were some who insisted that excessive use of whiskey was at the root of poverty

A fine study of aid and attitudes toward the poor to 1925 may be found in *From the Depths* by Robert H. Bremner (New York: New York University Press, 1964), upon which much of this section is based.

and that if the poor would only stop drinking they would no longer be poor. Some reformers also quite properly saw the connection between slums and the spread of disease and epidemics. They realized that the foul and filthy conditions under which the poor lived were breeding places for disease. Of the slums, Horace Greeley wrote in 1862, "In those places garbage steams its poison in the sun; there thieves . . . congregate and are made . . . there disease lurks and there is the daily food of pestilence plague awaiting its coming."[14] But here, too, it was not really the poor or their poverty that were the focus of attention. Instead, there was fear that unless these slum conditions were improved, the rest of society would be overrun by plague and disease. Such epidemics of smallpox, typhoid, and cholera were menaces to the public health, and in attempting to save the poor, the reformers were in large measure also saving themselves.

Probably the most enduring attitude toward the problem of poverty was that the poor should not be made too comfortable in it. There was serious concern that any real kindness or generosity shown the poor would merely encourage poverty and that the poor would come to enjoy it. Thus, aid was to be grudgingly, even meanly, given. Its narrow aim was "to prevent starvation and death from exposure as economically as possible."[15] Under these circumstances, so-called aid to the poor took a variety of forms, none of which came to grips with the roots or causes of poverty. Able-bodied children and sometimes adults were "bound" to more solid citizens for whom they would work. At other times, the poor were aided in their homes through gifts of coal or the payment of rent. Probably the most characteristic form of public help during the nineteenth century was the public poorhouse for the social discards from all walks of life. The young and the aged, the

GIVING FOOD

In the past it was thought that too much generosity shown the poor would encourage poverty. These nineteenth-century etchings show the poor of New York City receiving food and underground lodging (Culver Pictures)

insane and the feeble, the blind and the lame, the
orphan and the widow were all housed in a single
building, supported at the barest level of subsistence
possible by local communities. So scandalous did conditions in the poorhouses become that, during much
of the last quarter of the nineteenth century, demands for reform grew. However, the question was
how to help the inmates of these homes. On the one
hand, it was thought shameful that such vile conditions
should continue to exist; on the other hand, there was
a feeling that to make them better would encourage
pauperism. "The reformers wished to improve the poor
houses, but not to such an extent that people would
cease dreading to be sent to them."[16] Since the poorhouses were supported by public funds, those who
urged reform began to look to private charity as the
way out.

The early private charitable organizations had a
twofold purpose. They were to review applications for
help and to determine which among the so-called de-
serving poor were to be aided. Second, they began to
furnish financial aid themselves. But, as in public assistance, private charities were equally concerned that
their aid should not be so generous as to encourage the
poor. They still believed that a person was poor because of a defect in character or ability. Extended case
studies of those who applied for assistance provided
valuable information leading to a newer and more
humane view of poverty. As information about the
poor accumulated, those in private charity began to
realize that it was not a character defect that was
responsible for the poor, but the conditions of industrial
society. Once this view became more widely accepted,
the way was paved for a more realistic approach to the
underlying causes of poverty.

How Has Our Attitude toward the Poor Changed?

While old beliefs do not die easily, today it is more widely realized that most poor people are not poor because they want to be. Government has gradually come around to the view that most of the poor among us suffer from poverty through no fault of their own. If they are jobless, it is not because they are lazy but because there are no jobs. If there are drunkards or narcotics addicts among them, it is because they are poor, not because they are weak in character.

Today, it is generally recognized that one-fifth of the nation is poor because of a combination of social and economic circumstances. Many are poor because racial discrimination has' effectively limited jobs and educational opportunities open to them. Others are poor because of the geographic area in which they live, or because they are too sick, too old, or too young to work. Some are poor because the family has been broken up through separation or death of one of the parents and there is no wage earner in it. Some lack education and skills necessary for an industrial society, and so remain poor.

The overriding characteristic of poverty in America today is that it has resisted those efforts that have been made to eliminate it. The poor among us have not benefited as much as they should from general improvement in the economy as a whole. They have not participated in the general prosperity of the nation. A nation's general growth is measured by its Gross National Product. This is the total value of all goods and services produced during a given period of time. It is a rough measure by itself, and prices at the time must be taken into account. The Gross National Product was about $300 billion in 1950; it is over $800 billion

In 1967 half of all American families had a yearly income of more than $8,000. But for 25.9 million poor people (those with incomes of $3,300 or less for a family of four) the "American dream" of prosperity, a suburban house and a car, remains a myth (Wide World)

today. It is a sign that the wealth of the nation has increased substantially; but for the poor, little if anything has changed. They are just as poor as they ever were, and there are at least as many of them as there were before. Some say that, relatively speaking, since 1950 the poor have become even poorer.

We are beginning to realize that the curse of the poor is their poverty; that is, because they are poor they have little chance of improving themselves. Most families who are poor have been poor for a long time. Most children of the poor can expect to remain poor. Those with small incomes cannot move from where jobs are scarce to where jobs are plentiful. Their budget does not permit them to pay for transportation or the costs of moving and settling down in a new community.

The poor cannot give their children the education for the know-how and skills needed in our society. Even free public schooling costs money. Children have to be at least comfortably dressed with underwear, shirts, and shoes before they can even venture out into the streets to go to school. The clothes have to be appropriate to the climate in which they live. Children of the poor often do not have even the minimum amount of clothing needed to attend school, and so they stay home. They stay home, and poverty takes hold in their generation. Children of the poor need to have a good breakfast before they can even begin thinking about reading, writing, and arithmetic. This is why many schools provide such breakfasts and lunches. Yet because too many children of the poor are undernourished, they are unable to take advantage of such schooling as may be available.

The poor are more subject to illness and disease, and this causes them to lose such income or job opportunities as may exist. Because they are poor, because they have been poor for a long time, many of the poor see no way out of their poverty. The future looks blank and hopeless. The hopelessness of the parents is passed on to the children from generation to generation. A large percentage of the poor presently receiving aid come from families which also received aid. Because of these "facts of poverty," we have increasingly come to realize that the poor cannot be expected to improve themselves through their own efforts alone. Instead, they must be assisted in such ways that they, or their children, will gradually find themselves off the relief rolls and on the payrolls in some productive jobs.

Moreover, we have come to understand that to have

Education is a necessity for survival in our society today. But the children of the poor, undernourished and ill-clad,

often cannot take advantage of free public schooling, and so perpetuate the poverty of their generation (OEO)

a large number of poor people in an otherwise rich society is not only unnecessary but endangers that rich society as well. Those who are unemployed do not buy the goods and services they need. This contributes to loss of business and further unemployment. Poverty breeds disease which endangers the health of the entire community. Poverty breeds slums which not only infect their inhabitants but become, in turn, breeding places for crime and delinquency. We have come to understand that poverty affects even the ability of children to learn well at school and to develop those skills that are needed for future progress and for jobs. But how much assistance should be given to the poor? Does the responsibility for the poor rest mainly on the city, state, or federal government? What should be the role, if any, of private charities? Perhaps most important of all, what form should assistance to the poor take? These questions make the riddle of poverty in an affluent society even more difficult.

How Have Our Efforts to Help the Poor Changed?

Because of the change in the attitude toward poverty, there have been notable shifts in efforts to relieve the burden of the poor. For one thing, while private charity remains, public assistance by national, state, and local government is far more important. And while state and local assistance is considerable, today the federal government is the single most important factor in providing relief for the poor. There is another basic change. In the past, charity was given only to prevent death from starvation or exposure to cold; today there is an effort to provide the poor with enough aid so that they can begin to work their way into the mainstream of our economic life and eventually benefit, without further help, from the general prosperity of the nation.

The United States began to help the poor in a significant way rather late. There are many reasons for this. For one thing, during most of the nineteenth century there was cheap or free land on the frontier. This was regarded as a "safety valve" for the poor. They might, so it was thought, leave the city with its poverty, slums, and disease to begin life anew in a land of opportunity on a frontier that needed them. This frontier as a "safety valve" was more a vision of what might be than the reality of what it was. In truth, the poor could not pay their way to the frontier, and the urban poor lacked the skill that frontier farms required. Nevertheless, the persistence of the myth was enough to delay taking effective measures for the poor.

In industry, too, the United States was growing rapidly. Unlike Europe which had more workers than were needed, the United States had too few. Jobs, so it seemed, were always plentiful, and labor, so it seemed, was always needed. Indeed, the shortage of workers encouraged European immigrants to cross the Atlantic to take jobs in America's mines and factories and on the railroads. While wages were low and living conditions far from wholesome, nevertheless the lot of most immigrants was substantially better than it was in Europe. This blinded us to the needs of the poor among us and further delayed taking effective measures to help them.

It took the Great Depression of 1929 to arouse the government of the United States to its responsibility to the poor and deprived. A depression is the name given to business conditions in which there are rapidly falling prices, falling production of goods and services, rising unemployment, limitations on credit and expansion. It may be said that the depression was caused by the fact that prosperity, which was believed to exist in the country during the years before the depression, was

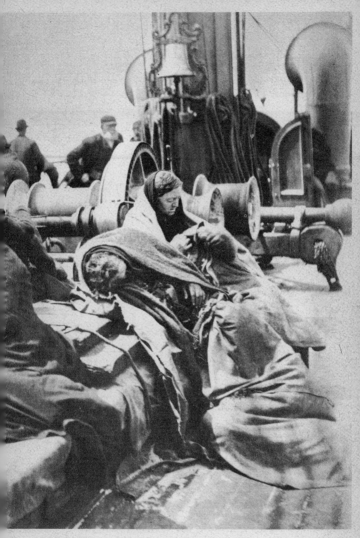

The needs of growing industry for labor in the early 1900's encouraged European immigration to the "golden land of opportunity" (Byron Collection, Museum of the City of New York)

unevenly shared; that is, neither farmers nor workers
were experiencing prosperity as much as they should
have been. Because neither workers nor farmers had
the money with which to buy the things they needed,
the supply of goods was larger than the ability of
farmers and workers to buy them. Making matters
worse was the failure on the part of government to
regulate the buying and selling of stocks* on the stock
exchanges of the country. Such failure caused prices
to rise to unreasonable heights. Men and women who
knew little about stocks bought them in hopes of getting
rich quickly. When stock prices began to fall violently
and suddenly on Tuesday, October 29, 1929, as a
result of a mammoth sellout by big stockholders who
lost confidence that America's prosperity could last any
longer, many of the middle class lost their savings.
Because many had borrowed in order to buy the stocks
in the first place, they were now in debt and impoverished.

The depression that began in October, 1929, never
really ended. The Second World War broke out before
it was really over. It was only the increased production
that World War II required that brought the depression to a close. While the 1929 depression was world-
wide, no nation was hit harder by it than the United
States. Poverty was widespread. Sixteen million lost
their jobs. This was about one-third of the work force.
The New Deal measures of Franklin D. Roosevelt,

---

stocks—shares in the ownership of a corporate business.
Such stocks, or shares as they are called, are traded in
stock exchanges. The biggest is the New York Stock
Exchange located on Wall Street in New York City.
The price of a share of stock is decided by what people believe the prospects of good earnings or profits for
the buyer are likely to be.

elected President in 1932, did much both to provide temporary relief for the needy and to set the tone for a more long-range solution to the problems of poverty.

President Roosevelt attacked the problems of depression and poverty vigorously. As never before in our history, government finally committed itself to provide relief for the poor and jobs for the able. Some laws, such as the establishment of the Civilian Conservation Corps and the Public Works Administration, sought to

During the Depression billions of dollars were spent for Public Works. This photograph illustrates a typical project (New York Public Library Picture Collection)

provide temporary jobs, but the main effort was to create permanent jobs where none existed by rein-vigorating the economy. More permanent laws came in the form of the establishment of the Securities and Exchange Commission which was designed to regulate the purchase and sale of stocks so that small stockholders would not suffer from lack of adequate information or cheating designed to make a few big stockholders rich.

Probably most important of all was the passage of the Social Security Act in 1935 which set aside a guaranteed income for each worker after the age of sixty-three. The income was to be supported by payments made to a special fund by workers, employers, and government. Since 1935 the number of workers covered has been expanded, the payments have increased, and the age at which eligible members can collect their social insurance has been reduced. About 90 percent of all jobs today are covered by social security. Special provision has also been made for widows and orphans, and, in recent years, medical insurance has likewise been tied to social security.

The system of social security remains a basic element in our effort to attack the problem of poverty, but it applies to only a limited group. Each worker is simply buying and paying for security in his old age. Social security is not charity. It is not designed for the poor alone. Most self-employed merchants and professional people are now covered by it. Because all workers must contribute to it, they are not getting something for nothing.

In addition to social security, federally assisted but state administered unemployment compensation laws were passed to provide income for those who lost their jobs through no fault of their own. Accident insurance was designed to give help to those who get hurt while working. Minimum wage and hours laws, as the name

Depression scene: Two of New York's many unemployed who earned their daily bread by selling apples on the streets (Wide World)

tells us, were designed to provide a floor beneath which wages would not fall and a ceiling beyond which hours would not go. In addition, under social security, special provisions were made for aid to the aged-needy, dependent children, blind and disabled adults, as well as to crippled children. Most of these programs are run by the states, bought and paid for largely from federal funds which provided some 90 percent of the money spent by states for such purposes.

Programs such as these are designed largely to prevent poverty from hitting new victims. They can help mainly those who have jobs or who have held jobs for a considerable period of time. Franklin Roosevelt spoke about one-third of the nation that was ill-housed, ill-fed, and ill-clothed. Social security and related measures have probably helped reduce this amount to one-fifth, the 20 percent who are the "invisible" poor. However, in that one-fifth are those who have never held jobs. How can the Negro be helped when discrimination has kept him from a job? How can the widow be aided when during the course of her life she has seldom been on a payroll? How can the dropout be helped when he left school before he could even qualify for a job? What help for the migrant from Puerto Rico and the South? What help for the migrant Mexican worker? What help for those in Appalachia—both urban and rural—who have long since forgotten what it means to work? It is because of the persistence of this hard core of poverty that Presidents Kennedy and Johnson urged a "war on poverty."

What Is Today's War on Poverty?

The year 1964 may be taken as the year in which a war on poverty was declared. Not that nothing had been done before, but it was in that year that the Congress, at the urging of President Johnson, provided the means and the funds needed to begin the fight. The enemy had long been identified. The weapons had long been at hand. But while poverty seemed a powerful enemy, the weapons seemed weak and ineffective. In 1964 two laws were passed which, it was hoped, would begin to make a difference. The first of these was the Civil Rights Act. The second was the Economic Opportunity Act.

The subject of civil rights is treated in another volume in this series, and so we will not go into detail about it here. However, it is well to remember that civil rights is just as much an anti-poverty measure as it is an effort to protect minority groups from discrimination. It has long been recognized that discrimination is a serious hurdle that minorities such as Negroes, Puerto Ricans, and Mexicans have had to overcome if they were to have equal access to jobs, housing, and education. As such, it is a vital weapon in the war against poverty.

The programs to end poverty, as provided in the Economic Opportunity Act, are many and varied. Its title tells us that its aim is less the direct relief of poverty than it is to help the poor to help themselves to a chance to participate equally in the prosperity of the country. Toward this goal the Economic Opportunity Act established the Office of Economic Opportunity (OEO) which provides, among other things, for the following:

THE JOB CORPS. The aim of this program is to provide education and training for young adults between the ages of 16 and 21. Young men and women who are both out of work and out of school are sent to residential camps in rural and urban centers. These centers are run by private industries or universities under contract with the OEO. They are designed to provide its students with living, learning, and working experience that will enable them to get and keep a good job.

THE COMMUNITY ACTION PROGRAM. As its name tells us, this aspect of the war on poverty is to encourage the poor to participate in their local communities in the effort being made to end poverty. The emphasis here is on local initiative and local suggestions with the intent of encouraging the poor to act and to speak for themselves. Its purpose is to encourage the poor to think of ways in which poverty might be ended and to apply for funds with which to begin the carrying out of ideas they have had. It is partly because "only the poor can know poverty" that they have been invited to plan and to apply for funds for remedial education for schoolchildren, pre-school programs for the nursery-age group, literacy and consumer education programs for adults. In this program the poor were to think of the idea, to apply for the money, and to have an important voice in spending it.

VISTA. Essentially this is a domestic Peace Corps. In it, volunteers participate without pay in programs to help the poor. The volunteers work directly in slum and ghetto communities in an effort to determine what the poor need and to help them get it. The program of Volunteers in Service to America (VISTA) has been a bold and imaginative step in the direction of helping the poor. It has helped to make the poor more

The Job Corps at Camp Kilmer, N.J., provides learning and working experience in electrical wiring (OEO)

Neighborhood people meeting outside to plan community action (OEO)

Vista volunteers serve for one year in the War on Poverty. They work directly in poverty-stricken communities with local agencies (OEO)

visible and to relate the problems of poverty with those of society.

This does not by any means exhaust the programs sponsored directly, or indirectly, by the Office of Economic Opportunity. Several cabinet departments, such as those of Health, Education and Welfare, Agriculture, and Labor, have all been brought into the struggle. When the activities of the OEO are added to those of the social security program and its related activities, the food distribution program run by the Department of Agriculture, assistance in public housing, to say nothing of the many programs in education in such poverty areas as Appalachia, one can readily see that a massive attack is being made against poverty.

The massive program launched to fight poverty grows out of the feeling that in twentieth-century America, poverty is inexcusable. Is the program massive enough? Has it come too late? Will it do the job intended for it? Answers to such questions are difficult to determine, and the program is still too new for reaching permanent conclusions. Certainly the race riots in Newark, Cleveland, and a host of cities duuring the summer of 1967 indicate that progress has been too slow and that the war against poverty has come too late. Deep and continuing anguish over houses unfit for people to live in, schools which have been unable to provide adequate progress in reading, jobs which have been unavailable, certainly are among the factors that have led to a developing pattern of violence in the slums of the cities of America. The poor are determined to be poor no more, to be invisible no more. They seek to capture political power and to use it in their interest. While the problems of poverty cannot be solved in a day, or in a year, the real question is, "Are we on our way?" And this, no one really knows. You will have to try to decide for yourself.

Part Two

Selected Readings

The selection below attempts to provide an insight into what poverty means in everyday terms. Consider: What connection is there between poverty and education? Between poverty and crime? What future is there for the two boys in this reading?

1. The Shame of a Nation

by PHILIP M. STERN *and*
GEORGE de VINCENT

"**I** got a lot of ideas, but I got a brick wall standing in my way, and soon my ideas is going to fade."

John Ash is talking. A moody boy of seventeen with ambition in his heart and poetry on his tongue.

John is a dropout, but he doesn't fit the stereotype.* Let him show you the books he's been reading: Bar-

---

stereotype—the standard mold.

From *The Shame of a Nation* by Philip M. Stern and George de Vincent (New York: Ivan Obolensky, Inc., 1965), pp. 85–89. Copyright © 1965 by Philip M. Stern and George de Vincent. Reprinted by permission of Astor-Honor, Inc., New York, N. Y.

bara Ward, James Baldwin, Charles Dickens* (fished out of a garbage pail), a book on semantics.*

John is a dropout by necessity, not by choice. His girl is pregnant. ("My father tried to teach me about sex . . . but I didn't listen, and now I got a family coming.") For him, school is finished. For him, it's go to work (*if* he can get a job) and get married.

The place John calls home is an unlikely place to find Dickens, Barbara Ward and a book on semantics. You get to it by walking down six worn wooden steps from the ghetto street, through a steel fire door, and into a basement corridor: narrow, dingy, brick-lined, bare-bulb lit. The corridor soon widens into the room where the "super" keeps the trash cans and other building paraphernalia. (John's cramped four rooms: there's a bureau and some chairs, and a dirty rug on the floor.)

By the side of the corridor, you find the undersized Ash apartment, and the ghost of John's near-past; his younger brothers and sisters. In the television commercial which monopolizes their attention, a white child tempts them with toys they will never enjoy. ("You'll *love* getting outfits for Barbie and Ken to go with the ones for Alan and Midge.")

For John's brother, Calvin, age eleven, reading is a tortuously slow affair, in which punctuation is unnoticed, the word "gentle" unfamiliar, and the word "photograph," when sounded for him, a surprise. ("It doesn't have any f's in it!" he exclaims.) Nathaniel's

---

Barbara Ward—a prominent economist; *James Baldwin*—the well-known Negro writer, author of *Another Country; Charles Dickens*—nineteenth-century English author, famous for his novels of reform and social protest such as *Hard Times*.

semantics—language.

Slum children play happily in the back alleys of the tenements, unaware of a world beyond the ghetto (OEO)

only playground is the street. ("Yeah, there's a park around here, but my friends say there's a red lady there and if she scratches you on the neck, you'll die. So I don't go to the park.")

Calvin's older brother, John, has an ambition: to start a youth labor union, so that kids in the ghetto will have some bargaining power when they go to work. But no one's going to pay John for starting a union of kids. And he's got to get paid. He's got to get a job. He's got a family on the way. ("I need a job, but I ain't got the schooling.")

You sense John will keep on plugging away. But he doesn't know what to do about that brick wall in front of him.

He's afraid all his ideas, all his ambitions, are going to fade. But he'll keep plugging.

"You try to move a little faster," he says, "so the world won't leave you behind with your head in your hands."

*   *   *

The most striking thing about Little Joe is his eyes. You take a close, hard look at them. Those are not the eyes of a thirteen-year-old. In other respects—in size, in movement—Little Joe is thirteen. But those eyes—hard, cunning—belong to a person of, what? twenty-one? thirty?

Little Joe is precocious* after a fashion. At thirteen, he is already an alumnus of Youth House, the detention home for young delinquents. He was put there, his mother says, for snatching money from a taxi driver —he and another boy.

And so at thirteen, Little Joe has a record. It will stick to him like his shadow the rest of his life. ("Ever been arrested, son?" "Yes, sir." "Well, we'll call you if we have any openings.") The ghetto is full of men and boys with records who willingly share their tales of futility and self-pity with the likes of Little Joe. And so, as far as he can see, Little Joe is all washed up. At thirteen.

---

precocious—knows a lot, although still young.

(Black Star)

Has he learned a lesson from his month in Youth House? "Not too good," his mother says. Afternoons, you are likely to find those hard eyes of Little Joe looking for a game of blackjack, roaming the streets with a pack of boys, mostly older than he is, a deck of cards and a couple of dollar bills in his pocket.

Visit Little Joe's home and you'll get some clues to his juvenile precociousness. Walk up the five flights, the eighty-five steps; approach the metal door to Little Joe's apartment. Just outside that door, another flight of steps leading to the roof, and bearing the tell-tale signs of a "shooting gallery" where junkies* "take off." . . . This is what Little Joe has grown up with, he and his eight brothers and sisters. And it's what the unborn brother or sister . . . will grow up with, too, because no one is going to do anything about this "shooting gallery" right outside Little Joe's door. (If a visitor can find the remains of that gallery, so could the police. But they don't.)

As is the case with one out of every three children in the ghetto, there is no father in Little Joe's home. You ask his mother what she tells her kids about what goes on outside that door. "You don't have to tell them nothing," she says. "They know. Even the little ones say, 'The junkies are out there again.'"

She'd like to get her kids out of there. For five years she's been applying to get into public housing—"the project," she calls it. "But they just write you and tell you you're still 'on the file.'"

. . . What's the future for these children? Little Joe's mother raises her eyebrows questioningly. "I don't know, really. That's what I wonder myself, sometimes."

---

junkies—dope addicts.

FURTHER INQUIRY

1. "I got a brick wall standing in my way," says John. What is the brick wall to which he refers?
2. In what ways are the problems of John Ash and Little Joe similar? How are they different?
3. How can a poor family have a television set? How do the commercials seem to make things worse?
4. Is a youth labor union a good idea? Why or why not? What kind of bargaining power does John want?
5. Why is John afraid his ideas and ambitions will fade?
6. Why will the record stick to Joe? Should it?
7. Why did Little Joe learn little of value from his stay at Youth House?
8. Why is getting into a public housing project difficult? What benefit might Joe's mother enjoy if she did get into one?

The Other America, probably more than any other book in recent years, alerted the nation to the problems of poverty in America. Consider: Why does Michael Harrington call the American poor "the other America"? Why does he say that poverty is invisible?

2. The Other America

by MICHAEL HARRINGTON

T H E millions who are poor in the United States tend to become increasingly invisible. Here is a great mass of people, yet it takes an effort of the intellect and will even to see them.

I discovered this personally in a curious way. After I wrote my first article on poverty in America, I had all the statistics down on paper. I had proved to my satis-

From *The Other America* by Michael Harrington (New York: The Macmillan Company, 1963), pp. 10–14. Copyright © 1963 by Michael Harrington. Reprinted by permission of The Macmillan Company.

faction that there were around 50,000,000 poor in this country. Yet, I realized I did not believe my own figures. The poor existed in the Government reports; they were percentages and numbers in long, close columns, but they were not part of my experience. I could prove that the other America existed, but I had never been there.

My response was not accidental. It was typical of what is happening to an entire society, and it reflects profound social changes in this nation. The other America, the America of poverty, is hidden today in a way that it never was before. Its millions are socially invisible to the rest of us. No wonder that so many misinterpreted Galbraith's* title and assumed that "the affluent society" meant that everyone had a decent standard of life. The misinterpretation was true as far as the actual day-to-day lives of two-thirds of the nation were concerned. Thus, one must begin a description of the other America by understanding why we do not see it.

There are perennial reasons that make the other America an invisible land.

Poverty is often off the beaten track. It always has been. The ordinary tourist never left the main highway, and today he rides interstate turnpikes. He does not go into the valleys of Pennsylvania where the towns look like movie sets of Wales* in the thirties. He does not see the company houses in rows, the rutted roads (the poor always have bad roads whether they live in the city, in towns, or on farms), and everything

---

John Kenneth Galbraith—author of *The Affluent Society*.

Wales—part of the United Kingdom which also includes England, Scotland, and Northern Ireland. Wales was made desolate by wasteful farming and mining methods.

Away from the modern highways of affluent America, poverty lies "invisibly" on the back roads. This shack is home to a family of Gila River, Arizona (OEO)

is black and dirty. And even if he were to pass through such a place by accident, the tourist would not meet the unemployed men in the bar or the women coming home from a runaway sweatshop.*

Then, too, beauty and myths are perennial masks of poverty. The traveler comes to the Appalachians in the lovely season. He sees the hills, the streams, the foliage—but not the poor. Or perhaps he looks at a run-down mountain house and . . . decides that "those people" are truly fortunate to be living the way they are and that they are lucky to be exempted from the strains and tensions of the middle class. The only problem is that "those people," the quaint inhabitants of those hills, are undereducated, underprivileged,

---

sweatshop—a factory with minimum safety conditions where workers work long hours for low pay.

When this train gets to 125th St. look out the window.

Give a damn.

This poster appeared on a New York commuter train as part of a campaign to make the middle-class suburbanite aware of poverty in the city's ghettos (New York Urban Coalition)

lack medical care, and are in the process of being forced from the land into a life in the cities, where they are misfits.

These are normal and obvious causes of the invisibility of the poor. They operated a generation ago; they will be functioning a generation hence. It is more important to understand that the very development of American society is creating a new kind of blindness about poverty. The poor are increasingly slipping out of the very experience and consciousness of the nation.

If the middle class never did like ugliness and poverty, it was at least aware of them. "Across the tracks" was not a very long way to go. There were forays into the slums at Christmas time; there were charitable organizations that brought contact with the poor. Occasionally, almost everyone passed through the Negro

61

ghetto or the blocks of tenements, if only to get downtown to work or to entertainment.

Now the American city has been transformed. The poor still inhabit the miserable housing in the central area, but they are increasingly isolated from contact with, or sight ·of, anybody else. Middle-class women coming in from suburbia on a rare trip may catch the merest glimpse of the other America on the way to an evening at the theater, but their children are segregated in suburban schools. The business or professional man may drive along the fringes of slums in a car or bus, but it is not an important experience to him. The failures, the unskilled, the disabled, the aged, and the minorities are right there, across the tracks, where they have always been. But hardly anyone else is.

In short, the very development of the American city has removed poverty from the living, emotional experience of millions upon millions of middle-class Americans. Living out in the suburbs, it is easy to assume that ours is, indeed, an affluent society.

This new segregation of poverty is compounded by a well-meaning ignorance. A good many concerned and sympathetic Americans are aware that there is much discussion of urban renewal.* Suddenly, driving through the city, they notice that a familiar slum has been torn down and that there are towering, modern buildings where once there had been tenements or hovels. There is a warm feeling of satisfaction, of pride in the way things are working out: the poor, it is obvious, are being taken care of.

The irony in this is that the truth is nearly the exact opposite to the impression. The total impact of the various housing programs in postwar America has been

_____

urban renewal—rebuilding of the slums and business areas of the inner-city.

Is the low-cost housing project a solution to the slums'
problems? The city's projects have become the scene of
crime and vandalism (Wide World)

to squeeze more and more people into existing slums.
More often than not, the modern apartment in a
towering building rents at $40 a room or more. For,
during the past decade and a half, there has been more
subsidization* of middle- and upper-income housing
than there has been of housing for the poor.

Clothes make the poor invisible too: America has
the best-dressed poverty the world has ever known.
For a variety of reasons, the benefits of mass production have been spread much more evenly in this area
than in many others. It is much easier in the United
States to be decently dressed than it is to be decently
housed, fed, or doctored. Even people with terribly
depressed incomes can look prosperous.

---

subsidization—financial help.

The aged represent a large segment of the nation's poor. Many old persons depend solely on social security and small pensions (OEO)

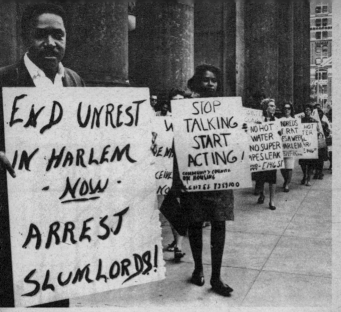

Rent strike: Only recently have slum-dwellers exerted political pressure to protest against abuses which they have long borne (Wide World)

This is an extremely important factor in defining our . . . ignorance of poverty. In Detroit the existence of social classes became much more difficult to discern the day the companies put lockers in the plants. From that moment on, one did not see men in work clothes on the way to the factory, but citizens in slacks and white shirts. This process has been magnified with the poor throughout the country. There are tens of thousands of Americans in the big cities who are wearing shoes, perhaps even a stylishly cut suit or dress, and yet are hungry. It is not a matter of planning, though it almost seems as if the affluent society had given out costumes to the poor so that they would not offend the rest of society with the sight of rags.

Then, many of the poor are the wrong age to be

seen. A good number of them (over 8,000,000) are sixty-five years of age or better; an even larger number are under eighteen. The aged members of the other America are often sick, and they cannot move. Another group of them live out their lives in loneliness and frustration: they sit in rented rooms, or else they stay close to a house in a neighborhood that has completely changed from the old days. Indeed, one of the worst aspects of poverty among the aged is that these people are out of sight and out of mind, and alone.

The young are somewhat more visible, yet they too stay close to their neighborhoods. Sometimes they advertise their poverty through a lurid tabloid story about a gang killing. But generally they do not disturb the quiet streets of the middle class.

And finally, the poor are politically invisible. It is one of the cruelest ironies of social life in advanced countries that the dispossessed at the bottom of society are unable to speak for themselves. The people of the other America do not, by far and large, belong to unions, to fraternal organizations, or to political parties. They are without lobbies of their own; they put forward no legislative program. As a group, they are atomized. They have no face; they have no voice.

Thus, there is not even a cynical political motive for caring about the poor, as in the old days. Because the slums are no longer centers of powerful political organizations, the politicians need not really care about their inhabitants. The slums are no longer visible to the middle class, so much of the idealistic urge to fight for those who need help is gone. Only the social agencies have a really direct involvement with the other America, and they are without any great political power.

To the extent that the poor have a spokesman in

American life, that role is played by the labor movement. The unions have their own particular idealism,
an ideology of concern. More than that, they realize
that the existence of a reservoir of cheap, unorganized
labor is a menace to wages and working conditions
throughout the entire economy. Thus, many union legislative proposals—to extend the coverage of minimum
wage and social security, to organize migrant farm
laborers—articulate the needs of the poor.

That the poor are invisible is one of the most important things about them. They are not simply ne-
glected and forgotten as in the old rhetoric* of reform;
what is much worse, they are not seen.

FURTHER INQUIRY

1. How can one who is not poor experience poverty?
2. Why have housing programs squeezed more
   and more people into existing slums?
3. Why is this isolation of the aged poor one of
   the worst aspects of poverty?
4. Why is poverty among the young more visible?
5. How can the poor win political power?
6. To what extent is a labor union a spokesman
   for the poor?

---

rhetoric—the art or style of speech making.

The former director of the Office of Economic Opportunity was a "General" in the fight to overcome poverty. Here he gives examples of how poverty affects different people. "Poverty is personal," says the author. Do you agree?

3. Poverty Is a Personal Thing

by SARGENT SHRIVER

T H E War on Poverty starts with individuals—with a man, a woman, a child—taking them one by one. But it does not stop there, because poverty is not just an individual affair. It is also a condition, a relationship to society, and to all the institutions which comprise society. Poverty is need. It is lack of opportunity. But it is also helplessness to cope with

From the opening statement to the Ad Hoc Subcommittee on Poverty of the House Committee on Education and Labor, April 12, 1965.

hostile or uncaring or exploitative institutions.* It is lack of dignity. It is vulnerability* to injustice. The treatment the poor get, at the hands of bureaucrats and politicians, at the hands of private industry, at the hands of landlords and merchants and agriculturists is more than the sum of the individuals involved. A pattern of response, a way of reacting to and treating the poor has become entrenched, and institutionalized.

Poverty is personal. But it is also a terrifyingly impersonal and dehumanizing condition, imposed on thirty-five million Americans. Both dimensions of poverty come through in this statement by Mrs. Janice Bradshaw of Pueblo, Colorado. It says a whole lot:

Poverty is a personal thing!

Poverty is taking your children to the hospital and spending the whole day waiting with no one even taking your name, and then coming back the next, and the next, until they finally get around to you.

Poverty is having a landlady who is a public health nurse who turns off the heat when she leaves for work in the morning and turns it back on at six when she returns. It's being helpless to do anything about it because by the time the officials get around to it, she has turned the heat back on for the day and then it will be off the next.

Poverty is having the welfare investigators break in at four o'clock in the morning and cut off your welfare check without an explanation, and then when you go down and ask, they tell you it is because they

---

exploitative institutions—conditions that unfairly take advantage of people.

vulnerability—openness to attack.

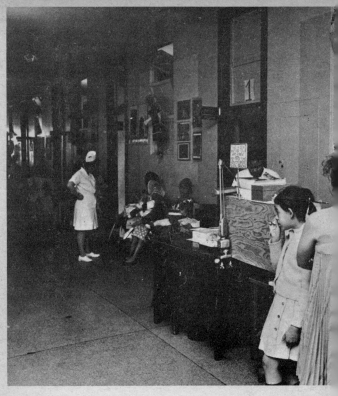

found a pair of man's slippers in the attic, where your brother left them when he visited a month ago. . . .

Poverty is having a child with glaucoma* and watching that eye condition grow worse every day, while the welfare officials send you to the private agencies, and the private agencies send you back to the welfare, and when you ask the welfare officials to refer you to this special hospital, they say they can't—and then when you say it is prejudice because

---

glaucoma—excessive pressure in the eye which can cause blindness.

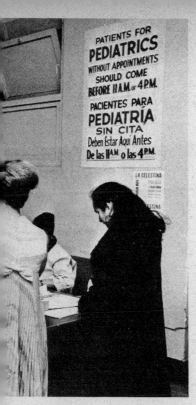

The poor are often at the mercy of bureaucratic, indifferent institutions. In a public clinic they can sometimes wait for days until seen (OEO)

you are a Negro, they deny it flatly and they shout at you: "Name one white child we have referred there." When you name twenty-five, they sit down, and they shut up, and they finally refer you, but it is too late.

FURTHER INQUIRY

1. Why do investigators break into the homes of the poor? What are they looking for?
2. Do you think that the poor are treated as people or as problems?

71

This excerpt attempts to provide some insight into what it is like to live on relief. It tries to show what it is like to have a welfare case worker investigate and decide how much one is entitled to have. Some of the standards are based on outdated attitudes toward poverty.

4. Family on Relief

by PHILIP DOUGHERTY

ANTONIA Matos is a tall, overweight, 26-year-old with a pretty face, large warm brown eyes, three small children and no husband. She is also a special sort of poverty statistic—an entry on the relief rolls.

Her family is one of the 389,000 defined by Welfare Commissioner James R. Dumpson* as "having only

---

James R. Dumpson—former Welfare Commissioner of New York City.

"Family on Relief: Study in Poverty" by Philip Dougherty, from *The New York Times* of April 5, 1964, p. 117. Copyright © 1964 by The New York Times Company. Reprinted by permission.

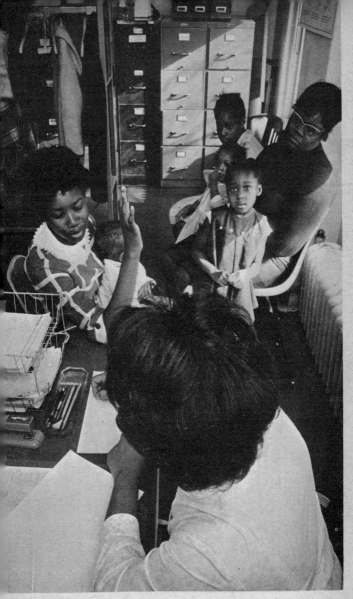

Mothers with no means of providing for their children apply for welfare benefits (OEO)

the necessities for subsistence."* Without the Department of Welfare she would be in subpoverty.

As it is, the $2,280.82 a year the family receives in welfare payments is $1,000 less than the "minimal budget requirement" called for by the Mayor's Council on Poverty in a report last week.

The only money that comes into the family's three-room apartment, which is badly in need of paint and floor covering, is a $94 check from the city every 15 days. Life depends on this check, on the monthly free Federal surplus foods* and free medical care.

The very existence of Miss Matos and her family, a 7-year-old son and two daughters, rests with her welfare investigator and his little black book—the omnipresent Manual of Policies and Procedures. The book tells the agent in minute detail what an individual's "entitlement"* is, depending on age, sex, employment and physical condition.

Exclusive of rent, utilities and a few other recurring items, the official daily budget, which is required by state law, comes to $1 for the mother, 90 cents for the son, 74 cents for the 4-year-old daughter and 66 cents for the baby. These allowances must provide food, clothing, personal care and household supplies.

The big days each month for Miss Matos in her rat-infested, fifth-floor walkup on East Fourth Street, are the 1st and the 16th. Those are the check days. Where she goes and what she does with the check depend a lot on the thyroid condition that keeps her

---

subsistence—barely living.

Federal surplus foods—foods said to be in greater quantity than can be sold are made available to the poor.

entitlement—the amount the person on welfare can be given.

Rats are a daily menace in many slum homes (Department of Health)

seriously overweight, the five flights that leave her breathless, and the children.

She goes just across cobblestoned, pushcart-filled Avenue C to the bodega* which she and other Puerto Ricans simply call "the Spanish store."

"The kids like Spanish food," she said. "Me, I eat half English and half Spanish." She likes the rice she gets there and the cans of Spanish beans, which she and the two oldest children have every day. She spends $25 for food every two weeks, which means she'll have meat five of the 15 days.

"I don't count welfare meat," she said, stroking Jean's curly head. Welfare meat and its kindred wel-

---

bodega—Spanish grocery store.

fare beans and welfare rice are the names used for the Federal surplus items.

Each month she gets about 19 packages of food with a retail value of $17.50—eight pounds of meat, two pounds of peanut butter, 10 pounds of flour, five pounds of cheese, four pounds of butter and two pounds of lard. There is also rice, cereal, cornmeal and powdered milk. Next month a pound of powdered eggs will be added.

The investigator arranges for the check-like voucher* for these staples. He also arranges for grants for such items as suits, overcoats and overshoes.

When the investigator visits he always checks on the receipts for rent and utilities. Many persons on relief fall behind on gas and electricity payments because the bills come bimonthly and they have failed to save for them.

"I don't owe nobody," Miss Matos said with pride.

The budgets worked out by the Welfare Department do not include such items as the 15 cents every couple of weeks for her son's milk and cookies at school, or the television set that takes the place of movies.

When the investigator works out the family budget he is guided by tables compiled by state home economists down to the last hairpin and bar of soap. Each family must be given a budget, although they do not have to follow it.

A welfare client must scrimp on the necessities for any luxuries. With Miss Matos, the luxury item is extra makeup.

"My face is something I don't fool around with," she said.

There is going to be an average of 5 percent in-

---

voucher—receipt.

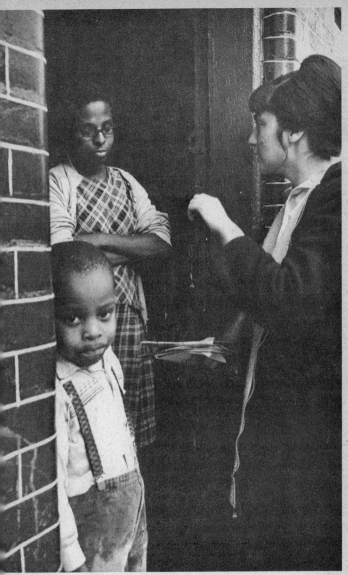

VISTA sends an investigator to whom clients must report all expenses (OEO)

crease to public assistance recipients on July 1. The other day, in the sudden darkness before a thunder-shower when her flat was looking its worst, Miss Matos was asked what she would do with $10 more in every check.

She surveyed the peeling paint, dirty wood floor, cheaply colored statues, pastel-print drapes, second-hand furniture—unrelieved drabness with the smell of poverty.

"Just look around," she said.

FURTHER INQUIRY

1. Should New York City tax its people to provide relief for new arrivals from Puerto Rico? Why or why not?
2. Should welfare payments be made more generous? If so, how much more? Justify your point of view.
3. Prepare a budget that you think would be appropriate for Miss Matos. Use the income she has.
4. Should Miss Matos be supported at a higher level? Why or why not?
5. Is it a sign of weakness that the poor fail to save for bills that come every month?
6. Should makeup be included in welfare allowances?

In this selection the author describes how it feels to come to the strange new world of the city. He also compares the problems faced by the poor who come to the city today with those of immigrants who came to the city fifty years ago. Consider: Why does the author say that the city has changed to the disadvantage of the newcomers?

5. Coming to the City

by BEN H. BAGDIKIAN

INTO the cities they pour, refugees from a silent revolution.

In Chicago the white folk from the countryside come mostly by Trailway bus, carrying all they own: a suitcase tied with rope, an old trunk, three shopping bags, a folded baby buggy, a bag of grits,* clutching

---

grits—coarse grain, hominy, a breakfast food.

From *In the Midst of Plenty* by Ben H. Bagdikian (Boston: Beacon Press, 1964), pp. 10–18. Copyright © 1964 by Ben H. Bagdikian. Reprinted by permission of Beacon Press.

a letter from a relative which came earlier with an address and a warning. "Don't take the cabs, they'll cheat you."

If they are colored they come mostly by that great iron artery in Southern Negro life, the Illinois Central Railroad, getting off in awe under the largest building they ever saw, carrying their old suitcases and trunks, cardboard boxes with clothes and pans, and they, too, have a carefully written address. . . .

If they are American Indians they may come in rickety old cars from the Dakotas and Utah and Arizona, fleeing the hunger of the reservations, making Chicago the fourth largest concentration of aborigines* in the United States.

They all gravitate toward the city, entering Chicago at the rate of fifty a day.

In a city as big as Chicago the newcomers face a strange new world. Old courage is not enough, previous skills meaningless, and what may have been minor disadvantages in education or family cohesion suddenly becomes catastrophic. It is possible, walking among the newcomers in their tenements, to hear these stories and these voices, and to see these sights:

"Why, this contract you signed says you have to pay carrying charges* for the furniture that are more than the furniture itself! Didn't you read this before you signed it?"

"Well, Sister, the man said it would be a small charge and I couldn't find my glasses that day."

"You mean you can't read, don't you?"

"Well, not very well, Sister."

---

aborigines—original inhabitants, Indians.

carrying charges—interest in the form of an additional charge for the privilege of buying merchandise on credit.

"Need money? No fuss—no red tape"—these signs put into print the torturing worries of the poor (OEO)

The twenty-four-year-old white girl, infant in arms, herding two other small children before her, has hitch-hiked continuously for two days and two nights from West Virginia and found her husband in the middle of Chicago during a blizzard, but when a social worker gives her applications to fill out and bus tokens to get to the agency for help, the girl, who has braved four hundred miles of the unknown, telephones five times in panic because the buses, the city, and the forms in triplicate are frightening.

"Mr. Donovan, my husband's back from jail so the welfare cut out my ADC* because I got a unreported male in the house. Does that mean my kids can't eat because their Daddy's home?"

At Stewart Elementary School in Chicago about one thousand students enter in the fall and about one thousand students leave before June because their parents have been evicted, have departed the district for another house, or have gone back South. A teacher said, "It's hard to teach a child much of anything in a school with a 100 percent turnover every year."

"Joe, you got to stay and help me. I need help."

"Ma, I'm going. I'm leaving for good. I don't know what I'll do but I can't stand it no more. I'm seventeen and I'll get along somehow. It's not my fault Pa's a drunk and you got eleven kids. Now you'll only have ten."

The heavy black pencilled letters, written large and painfully, are on grey cardboard tacked to the plaster in the damp corridor of 4860 North Winthrop: "Absolutely Do Not Throw Trash Out Bathroom Windows. Children Are Not to Run, Shout, or Play in Halls."

ADC—Aid to Dependent Children.

Eviction is a fact of life for the poor; unable to pay their rent, they move from place to place. Their children are seldom able to get the education that may boost them above the poverty level (OEO)

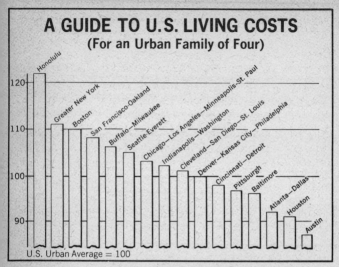

A GUIDE TO U.S. LIVING COSTS
(For an Urban Family of Four)

Honolulu
Greater New York
Boston
San Francisco-Oakland
Buffalo—Milwaukee
Seattle-Everett
Chicago—Los Angeles—Minneapolis-St. Paul
Indianapolis—Washington
Cleveland—San Diego-St. Louis
Denver—Kansas City—Philadelphia
Cincinnati—Detroit
Pittsburgh
Baltimore
Atlanta—Dallas
Houston
Austin

U.S. Urban Average = 100

Though the city may offer more employment opportunity for the rural immigrant, living costs are higher and many find it difficult to adapt to the fast pace of city life (Newsweek)

But it is not just Chicago. It is the same in New York, Los Angeles, Philadelphia, Detroit, Cleveland, Washington, St. Louis—all the great cities. In the last four decades a vast migration of 27,000,000 men, women, and children have flocked to the metropolis.* It is greater than the international migration which at its fullest flow from 1880 to 1920 brought 24,000,000 foreigners to America's cities. This time it is native Americans.

Almost all of them are poor. An alarming number of them remain poor for a long time.

The poverty of the newcomers is familiar and at the same time different. Prolonged lack of money can

_____

metropolis—city.

84

arise from a number of causes but whatever its cause it can have serious side effects that deepen the disease.

There are enormous differences in each person's response to adversity and because some people have been celebrated for personal triumph over poverty this has led to the assumption—usually by the well-fed— that to be poor makes one more noble. This was never true for most of the poor and it is not true now. Yet the belief persists that the poor compared with the affluent ought to be more honest, more resourceful, more puritanical, more disciplined, more resilient for the unskilled and the illiterate. It was a simple taneously more aggressive and more submissive.

They are not. Poverty is the pressure of living at the bottom of the social sea and this pressure finds the weakness in every personality. Poverty is dirty, vermin-infested, cold in winter, broiling in summer, and worst of all it is lonely. . . .

The native American poor of the 1960's are worse off in some ways than the foreign immigrants of two generations ago. Both came practically penniless, went into the worst housing, got the worst jobs, and suffered the isolation and discrimination that come to the impoverished stranger.

But the foreigners had their own culture and countrymen and history to give them assurance while they were being shunned by the new culture. In the old days if a man was disdained as a "Wop" or a "mick" or a "kike,"* he or his parents knew that there were a time and a place in which the Italians ruled the world and created a great culture, or the Irish wrenched freedom from the world's greatest power and defended their Roman Catholic faith, or the

---

Wop, mick, kike—slang terms for Italian, Irish, Jew.

Immigrants of 1910 came to America with strong cultural traditions and a commitment to the new land. They believed that poverty was a temporary condition (Jacob A. Riis Collection, Museum of the City of New York)

Jews shared the making of modern civilization and survived the suffering millennia* with learning and art. The lash of prejudice made its scars, as it always does, but there was some psychological solace* in one's own history and bitter satisfaction that the tormentor was so ignorant he didn't even know this history. . . .

---

millennia—thousands of years.

psychological solace—relief for the mind.

The foreign immigrant . . . also had a spur to drive him on. His was a total commitment to the new land: he had no way to leave. He could not hitchhike back to the farm, or take a bus to the home village, or go back ágain to the stream of migrant agricultural workers. Most had barely managed the ocean voyage here. There was no turning back.

They came from abroad at an opportune time. The New World was abuilding—railroads, canals, factories —and this was still done mainly by human hands. Pick and shovel required no diploma; there was work for the unskilled and the illiterate. It was a simple time of no application forms or Social Security* cards. . . . It was also a time for the small entrepreneur, the pushcart operator, the door-to-door peddler, the sidewalk salesman.

The modern American immigrant comes to the city at a bad time. The Negro and, to a lesser extent, the white rural migrant encounter discrimination harsher for coming from their own countrymen. From this the white man and the American Indian can usually retreat. There is a constant shuttling between farm and city, or reservation and city, in one direction when conditions at home get too grim, in the other direction when jobs in the city are too scarce. But the periodic retreats increase family instability, disrupt education, and prevent serious commitment to making a decent, permanent home. For the Negro there is no such easy return, since he escapes not only hunger but repression. Other conditions delay his setting down roots: an even lower level of education than the rural white, more discrimination against him with jobs and the

---

Social Security—a form of insurance for income during old age to which the worker, employer, and government contribute.

almost impermeable* barrier that keeps the Negro out
of the housing market.

The chief disadvantage for the native migrant is the
erosion of the traditional foothold for the novice* in
the metropolis: the unskilled job. The ditchdigger, the
factory hand, the street peddler—these were typical
roles for the newcomer starting upward from 1880 to
1920. But these are the jobs that are now shrink-
ing. . . .

The city itself has changed, almost entirely to the
disadvantage of the impoverished newcomer. The
transition from rural poverty to urban poverty is be-
wildering under any circumstances. The newcomer
probably came from dilapidated farmhouses or shacks
in the field without running water or electricity. In
1960 there were still 7,000,000 dwellings, 12 percent
of the total, that lacked running water or a toilet. In
the city a gas stove, plaster on the walls, electric wiring, plumbing, rigid rules of trash and garbage dis-
posal may be unfamiliar and seem unimportant. Life in
the city is almost always overwhelming. The lifetime
face-to-face personal relations of the village are replaced by fast-moving, fast-talking, impatient people in
business suits sitting in remote high offices requesting
forms in triplicate. Mass transit—subways, multiple
bus lines, transfers, endless blocks of huge buildings—
can be dizzying. The punctuality and impersonality of
city jobs can be depressing. The new legal and social
demands for proper clothing and medical care for
school children and the competition on the basis of
writing on school applications and job forms and wel-

---

impermeable—something through which it is not possible
   to pass.

erosion of the traditional foothold for the novice—wearing
   away or decrease of usual jobs for the beginner.

fare reports, all may seem mysteries comparable to the language barrier of the earlier foreigners and, in one way, worse. Most bureaucrats* assume that any native-born American can write the mother tongue, can fill out forms, understand rapidly-uttered directions in business protocol,* and can get around unaided in his own city. It is not a valid assumption. But few native migrants are willing to admit it. There is a glossary for the semi-literate—"I don't have my glasses with me," or "My hands are dirty, would you please fill it out?" or, "Oh, was I supposed to bring that paper with me?"—phrases used not only to avoid admission of difficulty with writing or reading, but also to avoid the painful moment when a parent has to admit to his own child that he is illiterate.

FURTHER INQUIRY

1. Why does the author call the poor "refugees from a silent revolution"?
2. Why is it hard to teach a child anything in a school where the turnover is high?
3. Why is there a great migration of people to the city?
4. Why is there a double standard that expects the poor to have a better character than the rich?
5. Why are the native poor worse off than the foreign poor of 40 years ago?
6. What differences would you expect to find between rural and urban poverty?
7. Is it the fault of the poor that they are poor?

_____

bureaucrats—a name given to those who work in the large government organizations.

protocol—proper style, here language.

Spanish Harlem in New York City lies between 96th and 130th Streets and between the East River and Central Park. It is made up largely of Puerto Ricans who have come to the city to live. Consider: "East Harlem is plain Jane," says the author. Why does she say this?

6. Spanish Harlem

by PATRICIA CAYO SEXTON

AT 6:30 A.M., while silk-stocking* Manhattan is asleep, East Harlem is starting to bustle. The poor are early risers. They have the jobs others don't want: the early-hour jobs, the late-hour jobs. Many rise early because it is a rural habit.

Along about 7:30 the streets are filled with fast-

---

silk-stocking—where the rich live, around Fifth, Park, and Madison Avenues.

From *Spanish Harlem* by Patricia Cayo Sexton (New York: Harper & Row, Publishers, 1965), pp. 1–4. Copyright © 1965 by Patricia Cayo Sexton. Reprinted by permission of Harper & Row, Publishers.

moving people: men, women, and swarms of children of all sizes. The parochial* school children can be seen in clusters, with their togetherness identity tag— a school hat, a blouse, a uniform.

You may be able to buy *The New York Times* at the corner newsstand in the morning, but you probably will not be able to buy a cup of coffee. The poor drink their⁻ coffee and eat their breakfasts, such as they are, at home. Few eat out.

Some will stand at the bus stops, but most will crowd into the downtown subways that speed them to jobs in commercial or silk-stocking areas; to serve the affluent, or work in their stores or small industrial shops. Many of the Negro women will go to domestic service; and the Puerto Rican women, to their sewing machines in the garment shops.

Later in the day, if it is warm, the men who have no jobs will come out and stand on the sidewalks and talk together. They will watch the street and the passers-by and kibitz with one another. The old people, and from time to time the housewives, will sit at the window and join the watchers. And those with leisure may call them idle. Later, when the children return from school, the sidewalks and streets will jump with activity. Clusters of men, sitting on orange crates on the sidewalks, will play checkers or cards. The women will sit on the stoop, arms folded, and watch the young at play; and the young men, flexing their muscles, will look for some adventure. Vendors, ringing their bells, will hawk hot dogs, orange drinks, ice cream; and the caressing but often jarring noise of honking horns, music, children's games, and casual

---

parochial—related to a church.

The streets of Spanish Harlem are always alive with activity, the stoops and sidewalks are playgrounds for the young and gathering places for the adults (Pictorial Parade; Stanley Sherer; OEO)

quarrels, whistles, singing, will go on late into the night. When you are in it you don't notice the noise, but when you stand away and listen to a taped conversation, the sound suddenly appears as a background roar. This loud stimulation of the senses may produce some of the emotionalism of the poor.

East Harlem is a busy place, night and day, filled with the joyous troubled lives of residents—rather than the heavy commercial traffic of mid-Manhattan. New York's street life is unique. So much action, so much togetherness. The critics who lament its passing have a point. The middle class who disdain life conducted so openly in the streets might compare its satisfactions to the sometimes parched and estranged quality of their own backyards.

East Harlem is a land of juveniles, especially in public housing. One of six residents of the area is under thirteen. One of four is under nineteen. As these children grow up and marry, they are likely to leave East Harlem, abandoning it to the aged and to new migrants with large families of small children.

The most striking contrast between the rich and the poor areas of Manhattan is in the visible wealth of the one and the visible children of the other. Also, there is the obvious restraint of the one and the expressiveness of the other. In East Harlem, music is everywhere, and visible gaiety, anger, fear, love, and hatred.

East Harlem is the poorest spot in one of the richest areas of the world, Manhattan. Across its southern border is the glitter of the east side gold coast, home of some of the world's richest and most celebrated people. On its west flank is another fabled area, Negro Central Harlem, off-and-on home of Adam Clayton Powell, A. Philip Randolph, James Baldwin, Malcolm X, Langston Hughes.

In contrast to such celebrities, East Harlem is plain

Jane. If it is "exotic," as advertising for middle income housing claims, that is because of the Spanish flavor below 125th Street. Almost half of its population speaks Spanish. As one of the world's largest Spanish communities, it has been a port of entry for the vast migration that has shuttled back and forth by air express from San Juan* to New York for two decades.

The spirited Latin music of East Harlem, pouring out from open tenement windows in every block, is Puerto Rican. Many signs, directions, conversations are in Spanish. The culture, the dark and tight style of dress, and the way of life, the store front pentecostal churches, the pleasantness and gentleness are among Puerto Rico's contributions to East Harlem.

East Harlem is special. Even the schools are special. They are tooled up with knowledge of the Puerto Rican language and culture, as they never were for other migrants. And the older groups say that the Puerto Ricans are coddled: "They never did it for us."

Italians, from an earlier immigration wave, and increasingly Negroes, who fill up the places not occupied by the Puerto Ricans, add other dimensions to the culture.

East Harlem is special because, except for a number of small Puerto Rican bodegas, it has few of Manhattan's accessories: gathering places, commerce, quaint little stores, office buildings, hotels. It is rather like a barracks, a place of residence for some 180,000 people—who populate a community big enough to call itself a city.

San Juan—capital of Puerto Rico.

FURTHER INQUIRY

1. How do you account for the existence of extreme wealth and poverty in big cities?
2. From this description, do you think Spanish Harlem is a pleasant place to live in or not?

Poverty may be defined in many ways. Indeed, it often goes unrecognized by the poor themselves. This is the true story (only the names have been changed) of the effects of poverty. Consider: How do people who were once prosperous become poor?

7. On the Brink of Poverty

by HERMAN P. MILLER

M R. Bacon at age thirty-eight was a temporary postal worker who made $1,820 in 1949. This was the total income he had to support his wife and three children aged six, four and one. The family lived in a low-income housing project, where they had a two-bedroom apartment costing $38 a month, utilities included. They were eligible for a three-bedroom apartment but did not apply for it in order to save on rent. The parents' bedroom was shared by their year-old daughter; the two boys had the other bedroom.

Mr. Bacon had quit school at sixteen. At seventeen he had been convicted of a petty theft and put on

From *Rich Man, Poor Man*, by Herman P. Miller (New York: Thomas Y. Crowell Company, 1964), pp. 60–61. Copyright © 1964 by Thomas Y. Crowell Company. Used by permission of Thomas Y. Crowell Company.

probation. He had knocked about from job to job, working as a construction laborer before he took the temporary job in the post office. He was a heavy drinker and, according to the social worker who reported the case, an unstable person who occasionally deserted his family.

Mrs. Bacon was more responsible than her husband, but she was having a very difficult time keeping her family together. She was a high school graduate but was unable to fulfill her plans for a nursing career. She had worked in a factory and in a hospital for a few years before her marriage. She was basically healthy, but at age thirty-seven all her upper teeth had been removed and she could not afford dentures. According to the social worker, Mrs. Bacon did a good job as a housewife, but she did not fully appreciate the seriousness of her plight. The apartment was described as pleasant and clean, with colorful curtains hanging on the windows. Mrs. Bacon managed her money well, although with only $20 a week to spend on food, cheese often had to be substituted for meat. The relationship between the parents was strained, but Mrs. Bacon thought her husband would stay home more if they could only get a television set.

The tension between the parents seriously affected the oldest child. He was asthmatic* and had to miss school one day each week to go to a clinic for treatments. At his young age, he had already been labeled a problem child in school and had to be taken to a psychologist.*

What happens to a family like the Bacons? The

---

asthmatic—having a condition in which breathing becomes difficult.

psychologist—one who attempts to diagnose learning and behavior problems.

seeds of poverty were planted here, not only for the present generations, but for future generations as well. Unfortunately, the family was not followed over the years, so there is no way of knowing just what became of them. Still it is interesting to speculate. Mr. Bacon had little schooling, no vocational training or skill, and he drank. None of these traits are conducive to regular employment or high income and it is likely that he has had neither. The Bacons may well be one of those families that would be counted among the poor at any time, but this is not necessarily the case. Life is complex and almost anything is possible.

In the years since the Bacons were first interviewed, much could have happened. The oldest child was twenty in 1963 and he could have been out working and contributing to the support of the family. If he had a factory job, he could be adding substantially to the family income. Moreover, the youngest Bacon child would be fifteen in 1963, if no other children were born. This would leave Mrs. Bacon free to accept employment and even a part-time job could pull the family above the poverty line. By considering only a few of the things that might have happened to this one family, you can see the factors that might cause the movement of families into or out of poverty over a period of time.

FURTHER INQUIRY

1. What factors would help the Bacon family rise above the poverty line? What factors would make them sink into it?
2. Do you think that Mr. Bacon deserved to be poor because he was a heavy drinker? Or would you say that perhaps he drank because he had a hard time supporting his family?

The Great Depression of 1929 may be said to have created relatively widespread interest in poverty as a social and economic problem. Consider: Why did it take a depression to awaken America to the problems of poverty? To what extent has our attitude toward poverty changed?

8. The Great Depression

by CAROLINE BIRD

"No one has starved," Hoover* boasted. To prove it, he announced a decline in the death rate. It was heartening, but puzzling, too. Even the social workers could not see how the unemployed kept body and soul together, and the more they studied, the more the wonder grew. Savings, if any, went first. Then insurance was cashed. Then people borrowed from family and friends. They stopped paying rent.

Herbert Hoover—President of the United States at the time the depression began.

From *The Invisible Scar* by Caroline Bird (New York: David McKay Company, Inc., 1966), pp. 27–30. Copyright © 1966 by Caroline Bird. Used by permission of David McKay Company, Inc.

In 1933, during the depression, thousands of unemployed lined up outside the State Temporary Employment Relief Administration seeking jobs (Wide World)

When evicted, they moved in with relatives. They ran up bills. It was surprising how much credit could be wangled. In 1932, about 400 families on relief in Philadelphia had managed to contract an average debt of $160, a tribute to the hearts if not the business heads of landlords and merchants. But in the end they had to eat "tight."

Every serious dieter knows how little food it takes to keep alive. One woman borrowed 50¢, bought stale bread at 3½¢ a loaf, and kept her family alive on it for 11 days. Every serious dieter knows how hunger induces total concentration on food. When eating tight, the poor thought of nothing but food, just food. They hunted food like alley cats, and in some of the same places. They haunted docks where spoiled vegetables might be thrown out and brought them home to cook up in a stew from which every member of the family would eat as little as possible, and only when very hungry. Neighbors would ask a child in for a meal or give him scraps—stale bread, bones with a bit of good meat still on them, raw potato peelings. Children would hang around grocery stores, begging a little food, running errands, or watching carts in ex-

Unemployed mill workers wait on a bread line in 1937 (Wide World)

change for a piece of fruit. Sometimes a member of the family would go to another part of town and beg. Anyone on the block who got hold of something big might call the neighbors in to share it. Then everyone would gorge like savages at a killing, to make up for the lean days. Enough people discovered that a five-cent candy bar can make a lunch to boom sales during the generally slow year of 1931. You get used

to hunger. After the first few days it doesn't even hurt; you just get weak. When work opened up, at one point, in the Pittsburgh steel mills, men who were called back were not strong enough to do it.

Those who were still prosperous hated to think of such things and frequently succeeded in avoiding them. But professional people could not always escape. A doctor would order medicine for a charity case and then realize that there was no money to pay for it. A school doctor in Philadelphia gave a listless child a tonic to stimulate her appetite and later found that her family did not have enough to eat at home.

A reporter of *The Detroit Free Press* helped the police bring a missing boy back to a bare home on Christmas Day, 1934. He and his friends on the paper got a drugstore to open up so they could bring the boy some toys. *The Detroit Free Press* has supplied Christmas gifts for needy children every year since.

A teacher in a mountain school told a little girl who looked sick but said she was hungry to go home and eat something. "I can't," the youngster said. "It's my sister's turn to eat." In Chicago teachers were ordered to ask what a child had had to eat before punishing him. Many of them were getting nothing but potatoes, a diet that kept their weight up, but left them listless, crotchety,* and sleepy.

The police saw more than anyone else. They had to cope with the homeless men sleeping in doorways or breaking into empty buildings. They had to find help for people who fell sick in the streets or tried to commit suicide. And it was to a cop that city people went when they were at the end of their rope and did not know what else to do. In New York City, the police

---

crotchety—cranky.

Christmas dinner in Iowa, 1934 (New York Public Library Picture Collection)

kept a list of the charities to which they could direct the helpless. In 1930 they took a census* of needy families, and city employees started contributing one percent of their salaries to a fund for the police to use to buy food for people they found actually starving. It was the first public confession of official responsibility for plain poverty, and it came not from the top, but from the lowest-paid civil servants, who worked down where the poor people were.

―――――
census—a count of the population.

Teachers worried about the children who came to school to get warm. They organized help for youngsters who needed food and clothing before they could learn. Sometimes Boards of Education diverted school funds to feed them. Often the teachers did it on their own. In 1932, New York City school teachers contributed $260,000 out of their salaries in one month. Chicago teachers fed 11,000 pupils out of their own pockets in 1931, although they had not themselves been paid for months. "For God's sake, help us feed these children during the summer," Chicago's superintendent of schools begged the governor in June.

FURTHER INQUIRY

1. What is a depression? Why do they occur? To what extent can they be avoided?
2. Should the poor be supplied with toys? Why or why not?
3. Why was responsibility for poverty first recognized by the lowest-paid civil servants rather than highly placed officials?

During the dark days of the depression, Franklin Delano Roosevelt was inaugurated for his second term as President. This excerpt from his address outlines both the problems before the nation and his hopes for the future. Broadcast over radio to the nation, it moved men as few speeches do. Today, the one-third poor of Roosevelt's day has become one-fifth of the nation. To what extent is this adequate progress?

9. I See One-Third of a Nation Ill-Housed, Ill-Clad, Ill-Nourished

by FRANKLIN DELANO ROOSEVELT

L ET us ask again: Have we reached the goal of our vision of that fourth day of March, 1933? Have we found our happy valley?

I see a great nation, upon a great continent, blessed with a great wealth of natural resources. Its hundred and thirty million people* are at peace among them-

---

people—the population of the United States is now more than 200 million.

From Franklin D. Roosevelt's *Second Inaugural Address*, January 20, 1937.

selves; they are making their country a good neighbor among the nations. I see a United States which can demonstrate that, under democratic methods of government, national wealth can be translated into a spreading volume of human comfort hitherto unknown, and the lowest standard of living can be raised far above the level of mere subsistence.

But here is the challenge to our democracy: In this nation I see tens of millions of its citizens—a substantial part of its whole population—who at this very moment are denied the great part of what the very lowest standards of today call the necessities of life.

I see millions of families trying to live on incomes so meager that the pall of family disaster hangs over them day by day.

I see millions whose daily lives in city and on farm continue under conditions labeled indecent by a so-called polite society half a century ago.

I see millions denied education, recreation, and the opportunity to better their lot and the lot of their children.

I see millions lacking the means to buy the products of farm and factory and by their poverty denying work and productiveness to many other millions.

I see one-third of a nation ill-housed, ill-clad, ill-nourished.

It is not in despair that I paint you that picture. I paint it for you in hope—because the nation, seeing and understanding the injustice in it, proposes to paint it out. We are determined to make every American citizen the subject of his country's interest and concern; and we will never regard any faithful, law-abiding group within our borders as superfluous. The test of our progress is not whether we add more to the abundance of those who have much; it is whether we provide enough for those who have too little.

One of President Roosevelt's solutions to unemployment was the Works Progress Administration, created by the government to combat nationwide poverty. It provided jobs—not simple relief. Work crews built dams, bridges, roads, and other public facilities (Wide World)

If I know aught of the spirit and purpose of our nation, we will not listen to Comfort, Opportunism, and Timidity. We will carry on.

Overwhelmingly, we of the Republic are men and women of good will; men and women who have more than warm hearts of dedication; men and women who have cool heads and willing hands of practical purpose as well. They will insist that every agency of popular government use effective instruments to carry out their will.

FURTHER INQUIRY

1. Do you think that a country's progress should be measured by its gross wealth or widespread distribution of wealth?
2. Compare this speech with that of Lyndon Johnson. What similarities and differences do you see? How do you account for them?

Walter Reuther, President of the United Automobile Workers of America, writes here of the rapid changes taking place in the automobile industry and the effect of these changes on problems of jobs and poverty. He observes that today we can invent machines faster than we can find jobs for those men who lose their jobs to the machine. What, if anything, should be done about this? Mr. Reuther tells us that "we must manage abundance by learning to share it." What does he mean? How might this be done?

10. Around the World in One Second

by WALTER P. REUTHER

I went to work in the Ford Motor Company in April of 1927, when they were producing the last Model T's. At that time it took three and a half weeks to machine a Model T engine block from the rough casting to the finished engine block, with tens of thousands of workers operating individual machines that performed individual operations. In 1950, Ford got its first fully automated engine line. The first plant was

From "First Things First," *An Occasional Paper on the Free Society* by Walter P. Reuther, 1964, p. 5, with permission of the Center for the Study of Democratic Institutions.

Automation means using machines to run machines, and unemployment for many unskilled laborers. This automated galvanizing line stretches for one-fifth of a mile (Bethlehem Steel Co.)

opened near the city airport in Cleveland, Ohio. When I went through it, a V-8 engine block . . . came from the foundry in the rough casting, an overhead conveyor fed it into the automated machine line, and without a worker's hand touching it, the engine block came out fourteen and six-tenths minutes later, fully machined.

112

When the people at Ford asked me what I thought, I said that obviously I was greatly impressed by the tremendous technological advance that this automated machine line represented as compared to the old Model T that I had learned on. The management-executive then asked whether I was not concerned about the fact that I couldn't collect union dues from all these machines. I replied that it wasn't this that bothered me; what bothered me, I said, was how Ford was going to sell cars to all these machines.

Now, in 1964, this automated engine line is already becoming obsolete.* It is built essentially around the computers that are used in all basic American industries. But there is a new computer on the drawing boards, which will be a thousand times faster than the ones now in use. The present computer has an impulse cycle of three-tenths of a millionth of a second; the new computer will have an impulse cycle of three-tenths of a *billionth* of a second. The present computer is housed in a room with a half-acre of floor space; the new one fits into a desk drawer.

I asked a friend of mine, who is one of the best mathematicians in the country, to give me a simple illustration that would indicate how fast three-tenths of a billionth of a second is. He said, "Well, if you wanted to walk around the world at the point of its greatest circumference, which is 25,000 miles at the Equator, and you took one average step each time this new computer can either give the machine a new instruction or work out another equation in a mathematical problem—in other words, if you took one step every three-tenths of a billionth of a second—you could walk around the world in less than one second."

These are the new dimensions. Obviously a society

---

obsolete—out of date.

Drawing by D. Fradon © 1964 The New Yorker Magazine, Inc.

'I see Fenton's is finally automating'

that has the scientific and technical ability to create these kinds of tools must also develop equal creative genius in giving social purpose to these tools. They are of no value otherwise. This is the gap between our progress in the physical sciences and our progress in the human and social sciences.

We have learned to create economic abundance because we have the tools of abundance. But we have not created the economic and social mechanisms within the framework of our free society that will allow us to manage abundance by learning to share it, by learning to relate it to the basic needs of the total community. There are 50,000,000 Americans living in poverty in America despite all the books about affluence. There are 50,000,000 Americans living below the level of what the government economists tell us represents the minimum of family income requirement. This is the area in which we are being challenged to demonstrate the worth and the quality of our society.

FURTHER INQUIRY

1. It has been said that new technology may make it unnecessary for all to work to make the things society needs. If men do not work, how will they have the money they need to support themselves?
2. What did Reuther mean when he asked: How was Ford going to sell cars to all these machines?
3. What do you understand by the gap the author claims exists between physical sciences and the human and social sciences?

Since hard-core poverty still exists in America, President Johnson urged a "war" against it. In this address he submits the Economic Opportunity Act of 1964 which was to be the major weapon in that war. The Act was designed to open, present, and advance new opportunities to the impoverished. How can provision for equal economic opportunity be made? What relationship exists between the war on poverty and equal economic opportunity? To what extent is civil rights legislation related to the war on poverty?

11. Message on Poverty

by LYNDON BAINES JOHNSON

WE are citizens of the richest and most fortunate nation in the history of the world.

One hundred and eighty years ago we were a small country struggling for survival on the margin of a hostile land.

Today we have established a civilization of free men which spans an entire continent.

With the growth of our country has come opportunity for our people—opportunity to educate our children, to use our energies in productive work, to

From the War on Poverty: *Economic Opportunity Act of 1964*, Senate Document No. 86, Washington, D. C., 1964.

increase our leisure—opportunity for almost every American to hope that through work and talent he could create a better life for himself and his family.

The path forward has not been an easy one.

But we have never lost sight of our goal—an America in which every citizen shares all the opportunities of his society, in which every man has a chance to advance his welfare to the limit of his capacities.

We have come a long way toward this goal.

We still have a long way to go.

The distance which remains is the measure of the great unfinished work of our society.

To finish that work I have called for a national war on poverty. Our objective: total victory.

There are millions of Americans—one-fifth of our people—who have not shared in the abundance which has been granted to most of us, and on whom the gates of opportunity have been closed.

What does this poverty mean to those who endure it?

It means a daily struggle to secure the necessities for even a meager existence. It means that the abundance, the comforts, the opportunities they see all around them are beyond their grasp.

Worst of all, it means hopelessness for the young.

The young man or woman who grows up without a decent education, in a broken home, in a hostile and squalid environment, in ill health or in the face of racial injustice—that young man or woman is often trapped in a life of poverty.

He does not have the skills demanded by a complex society. He does not know how to acquire those skills. He faces a mounting sense of despair which drains initiative and ambition and energy.

Our tax cut will create millions of new jobs—new exits from poverty.

With the help and concern of private industry and individuals, displaced workers can learn new skills (OEO)

But we must also strike down all the barriers which keep many from using those exits.

The war on poverty is not a struggle simply to support people, to make them dependent on the generosity of others.

It is a struggle to give people a chance.

It is an effort to allow them to develop and use their capacities, as we have been allowed to develop and use ours, so that they can share, as others share, in the promise of this nation.

We do this, first of all, because it is right that we should.

From the establishment of public education and land-grant colleges* through agricultural extension and

---

land-grant colleges—a milestone in higher education when in 1862 the Morrill Act was passed providing for the establishment of colleges which would serve the people of the state.

encouragement to industry, we have pursued the goal of a nation with full and increasing opportunities for all its citizens.

The war on poverty is a further step in that pursuit.

We do it also because helping some will increase the prosperity of all.

Our fight against poverty will be an investment in the most valuable of our resources—the skills and strength of our people.

And in the future, as in the past, this investment will return its cost many fold to our entire economy.

If we can raise the annual earning of 10 million among the poor by only $1,000, we will have added $14 billion a year to our national output. In addition we can make important reductions in public assistance payments which now cost us $4 billion a year, and in the large costs of fighting crime and delinquency, disease and hunger.

This is only part of the story.

Our history has proved that each time we broaden the base of abundance, giving more people the chance to produce and consume, we create new industry, higher production, increased earnings, and better income for all.

Giving new opportunity to those who have little will enrich the lives of all the rest.

Because it is right, because it is wise, and because, for the first time in our history, it is possible to conquer poverty, I submit, for the consideration of the Congress and the country, the Economic Opportunity Act of 1964.

The act does not merely expand old programs or improve what is already being done.

It charts a new course.

It strikes at the causes, not just the consequences of poverty.

It can be a milestone in our 180-year search for a better life for our people.

This act provides five basic opportunities:

It will give almost half a million underprivileged young Americans the opportunity to develop skills, continue education, and find useful work.

It will give every American community the opportunity to develop a comprehensive plan to fight its own poverty—and help them to carry out their plans.

It will give dedicated Americans the opportunity to enlist as volunteers in the war against poverty.

It will give many workers and farmers the opportunity to break through particular barriers which bar their escape from poverty.

It will give the entire Nation the opportunity for a concerted attack on poverty through the establishment, under my direction, of the Office of Economic Opportunity, a national headquarters for the war against poverty.

FURTHER INQUIRY

1. How can provision for equal economic opportunity be made? What relationship exists between the War on Poverty and equal economic opportunity?
2. To what extent is civil rights legislation related to the War on Poverty?
3. What is meant by the expression "War on Poverty"?
4. Is total victory in a War on Poverty possible? Why or why not?
5. How can one get trapped in a life of poverty?
6. What skills are required by a modern society? How can they be attained?

7. How does the attitude expressed here differ from the attitude toward poverty prevailing during the nineteenth century?

8. How will helping some increase the prosperity of all?

9. Why does the former President call the War on Poverty an investment in people?

The author of this article was Assistant Director of the Office of Economic Opportunity. Here he presents a summary of what the OEO has done as his partial reply to Saul Alinsky, a professional organizer of poor communities and a critic of the War on Poverty. Why does Mr. Bookbinder say, "There is nothing more important that has been done in behalf of the poor in this country than to give them a sense of belonging to the community . . ."?

12. What the OEO Has Done

by HYMAN H. BOOKBINDER

HERE is a quick report of what I think has happened in the War on Poverty so far:

First, the major battle, in my scale of values, has been won already. That major battle was to get American credibility, acceptance of the fact that we do have a disgusting problem of poverty in this country. The American people now believe what they didn't believe when Harrington first wrote his remarkable book *The Other America*. They know there is an "other America" of more than 20 million people living in abject

From *Communities in Action,* Vol. 1, No. 2, July, 1966 "Alinsky vs. Bookbinder," pp. 24–25.

poverty and they're beginning to do something about it. Secondly, there is greater understanding among all of us that poverty is no single, simple phenomenon that can be cured by a single, simple program or under a single slogan such as "organize for power."

There are many kinds of poverty in America; and they cry out for many many programs with each one to combat a special aspect or by-product of poverty. The poverty in the Baltimore ghetto is not the same as the poverty problems of Appalachia, and it is not the same as the poverty problems of young widows and divorcees with young children wherever they are. It's not the same as the poverty of the aged or of the American Indians or of migrant labor.

So many programs are needed. One of the greatest fallacies of some who are critics of this program is to think that the War on Poverty is OEO. Some critics are even more simple-minded and think the whole War on Poverty goes to the issue as to how many local residents serve on a CAP* board.

The fact is we're moving on many fronts. So the third major achievement in the War on Poverty thus far is that it has encouraged, it has inspired important action in many fields. Let me tick some of them off for you—the Appalachian Regional Commission Bill—over a billion dollars to start economic development; the Economic Development Administration—similarly a multi-billion dollar program; the first major break-through in Federal Aid to Education because it was poverty-oriented—more than a billion dollars; new programs in health and housing and Social Security improvements; Medicare,* which got the final push because it was in the context of the war against pov-

---

CAP—Community Action Program.
Medicare—federal government aid for the aged-ill.

Old folks sign up for Medicare benefits (Wide World)

erty; the Older Americans Act. All of these things are part of the War on Poverty.

This year, we'll see more action. We'll see an increase in the minimum wage; we'll see improvements, I hope, in unemployment compensation. The next victory in my book is that we've gotten all kinds of establishments moving. Yes, the establishment is a whole range of establishments. The League of Women Voters* is one part of the establishment. The labor movement is part of the establishment and the Federal establishment is part of the establishment; and we're moving them all. Just recently, the Bureau of Indian Affairs was basically

---

League of Women Voters—an organization designed to encourage political participation and to spread information about political candidates.

The Economic Opportunity Act of 1964 provided funds for the nation's underprivileged to develop skills and continue education—as in this Job Corps Center in Cherokee, North Carolina (OEO)

reorganized, prodded and stimulated by the understanding that comes out of the anti-poverty program.
The Agriculture Department in 1966 isn't the same
Agriculture Department that it was in 1960, or 1962
or even 1964. The United States Employment Service
is reorienting its work and is now more concerned
about the disadvantaged than it ever was before. The
Office of Education is moving with concern for the
disfranchised.* The Welfare Administration—why, two
years ago the social workers were ready to throw us
down the drain. Many of them still do but they've
made some adjustments we've forced upon them—and
we're a little bit friendlier than we were two years ago.

The educators of this country have had to make adjustments in their own standards of behavior, and
the labor movement has made some changes already.
These are important, if not calculable, advantages for
the War on Poverty. But now, let me get to the OEO
itself. We have now developed programs that you
know about. They are not good enough, they are not
reaching enough people but they already have begun
to touch in meaningful ways the lives of millions of
poor people. Our objective is not to make poor people
happier in their poverty but to get them out of poverty.
So we've had programs like Job Corps—a difficult,
back-breaking program but it's beginning to work, and
several thousand young men and women who a year
ago couldn't pass a physical exam or a mental exam
for the Armed Services now are either back in school,
in the Armed Services or on jobs. Six hundred thousand young men and women have already had Neighborhood Youth Corps jobs. Over fifteen thousand have
had work study assignments so they can continue going
to college. Upward Bound will reach twenty thousand

---

disfranchised—those without the vote.

difficult kids—difficult in terms of academic achievement—and help them get into college and stay there.
With Head Start—if we close shop tomorrow, I think
the lasting memorial to OEO, to the poverty program,
is that it has revolutionized the whole concept of pre-
school education and development work.

Now the major thing is OEO, the issue on which
Saul Alinsky and I agree. I stress that we agree. There
is nothing more important that has to be done on
behalf of the poor in this country than to give them a
sense of belonging to the community—that they are
the community—that they have something to contribute—that they can help determine their future. In
this area I pay my salutes to Mr. Alinsky. He's done
something in this area. But what he has done on a retail basis for 30 years with uneven results, we are
now doing on a wholesale basis with uneven results,
too. But we're beginning to move. Illustrating this—
8,000 men and women who two years ago were just
like any other people living and working and stultify-
ing in their respective communities are now recognized
community leaders, serving on their CAP boards, government councils, advisory councils. Next week, there'll
be more than 8,000, and next month, more than that.
Twenty-five thousand other poor people are working
for the poverty program as staff people, workers, coun-
selors, and advisors, working for the poverty program
and getting that sense of recognition as well as that
sense of participation and employment. This is a revolution that's going on in the anti-poverty program today.

FURTHER INQUIRY

1. About the programs of the OEO, Mr. Bookbinder says, "They are not good enough."
   What criticism does he have of his own program? How can the programs of OEO be improved?
2. Would you say that most Americans are now
   aware of poverty? What are your reasons?
3. To what extent may the War on Poverty be
   considered a revolution?

Part of the answer to poverty surely lies in teaching vocational skills to the poor. The Job Corps, sponsored by the Office of Economic Opportunity and operated both by colleges and by private corporations tries to do just this. Although there has been much controversy about the aims and methods of the Job Corps, it remains a massive, nation-wide attempt to combat poverty by providing the poor with marketable skills. The Job Corps has sometimes been described as the "last chance" for the poor. Why? To what extent does the Job Corps have a better chance to salvage the hopes and abilities of the poor than the schools themselves?

13. The Job Corps

by JOHN BAINBRIDGE

As we headed toward the dining hall, Mr. Kurth* told me that a Corpsman's day begins at six, when he's supposed to get up (if he doesn't get up on time, his group will probably sanction him), dress, make his bed and straighten up his room, and go to breakfast. Classes begin at eight-fifteen. Lunch is

---

Kurth—a Job Corps official mainly responsible for the morale of the Corpsmen.

"The Job Corps," by John Bainbridge, in *The New Yorker*, May 21, 1966, Vol. XLII, No. 13, pp. 112–158. Copyright © 1966 by *The New Yorker* Magazine, Inc. Reprinted by permission.

Job Corpsmen from Flatwoods conservation center in Virginia build a bridge leading to new picnic grounds (OEO)

served from eleven-thirty until twelve-thirty, and classes resume at twelve-forty-five and run until three-forty-five. If a Corpsman has vocational instruction in the morning, he has academic instruction, which consists of communications, math and science, and social studies, in the afternoon. He attends his group meeting from four-thirty until five-forty-five, and he goes to dinner at six. Afterward, he has free time until ten; he may go to the recreation hall, where he can shoot pool, play ping-pong, or, three times a week, see a movie, or he may go to the gym or take part in any of the several activities organized by the group leaders and instructors. Between ten and eleven, he helps in the cleanup of his dormitory, which includes mopping the floors. Lights are out at eleven. Twice a month, under normal circumstances, a Corpsman gets a weekend pass. During the month, he may also receive Saturday-night passes, and there are incentive programs that reward what Mr. Kurth calls "the real top kids" with weekday passes and other privileges. "As part of establishing a peer culture, we give these outstanding kids the title of Lead Corpsmen," he said. "We also now name a Corpsman of the Week and a Corpsman of the Month. Another honor is to get elected to the student council—or the House of Representatives, as the Corpsmen have decided to call it. One member is elected from each dormitory. Or you can be elected editor of the newspaper the Corpsmen are putting out, or of the yearbook they've started. These kids have never participated in things like this before. They can really mean a lot."

Across the road from the dining hall, Mr. Kurth stopped to introduce me to a very well set-up Negro in his late twenties named Charles Utley, who was carrying a clipboard and wearing slacks and a combination of handsome blue sweaters. He used to be called the Center's Truant Officer but he is now known as the Work Supervisor, which means that he is in charge of the Corpsmen who are put on work detail. His qualifications for the post include a ten-year hitch in the Army, where he was a squad leader in an airborne division and heavyweight boxing champion of the Far East. "I take care of the bad boys," he said. "If I see them sitting around, I get them to class or wherever they're supposed to be. The boys give me a lot of respect. They do what I tell them to do. They think I'm kind of a bogeyman. I don't like the reputation of being a bogeyman, but if that gets results, it's all right with me." . . .

I followed Mr. Kurth to a table in a corner of the [dining] room, at which a lean, neatly dressed Negro boy was sitting by himself. The boy, whom Mr. Kurth greeted as Willis, gave him a short but not unfriendly smile, shook hands with me, and went back to his meal, on which he remained quite intent. It developed during the rather one-sided conversation that Mr. Kurth struck up with Willis that the boy had decided to leave the Job Corps and go into the Army. It also became evident that Mr. Kurth had tried to persuade him to stay at Kilmer,* and had failed. He nevertheless asked Willis why he had decided to switch to the Army. "I just think I'll get more out of it," he replied. He finished eating, stood up, gave Mr. Kurth another short smile, said, "So long," picked up his tray, and left.

"He could be a powerhouse kid," Mr. Kurth said. "We just don't have enough here yet to challenge him. It's too bad. Earlier today, three other Corpsmen told me they were leaving. They're not the same kind of kids as this one, but you hate to see them go. One of them said there were too many rules here. Another

Kilmer—Camp Kilmer, New Jersey.

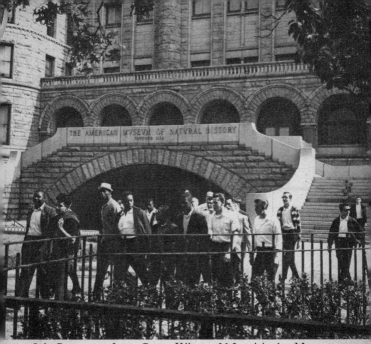

Job Corpsmen from Camp Kilmer, N.J., visit the Museum of Natural History in New York (OEO)

said he didn't like living with Negroes. The third one said, 'The guys at home told me not to go. They said I was getting into something I wouldn't like. These guys were right.' Which doesn't make much sense, but it's often hard to put your finger on the real reason they leave. Sometimes it's just homesickness. Nearly all the kids are homesick the first month. A few have it longer. Here again, a lot can be done through the groups. If there's a kid who wants to go home, the group leader knows about it. It's discussed in the S.C.G. [Staff Consultation Group] meeting, and they bring it up in the group meeting. They start to pressure this kid into staying by asking him what he's going home to. They tell him he's going back to the very thing he was trying to

133

get away from. Here, they tell him, is an opportunity, and they try to show him he should stay and take advantage of it. Of course, if a kid just wants to go home for a weekend to see his family—well, we're flexible. That's probably the hardest thing for the staff—to be flexible. But we've got to be, if we're going to handle the biggest problem we have here, which is being creative enough to find solutions to these kids' problems."

Recalling the case of the boy who had said he was leaving because he didn't like living with Negroes, I asked if racial feeling among the Corpsmen created a serious problem.

"No, it hasn't been a serious problem," Mr. Kurth replied. "Sure, we have a problem when a white kid calls a Negro kid a 'nigger.' It's bound to cause trouble, and could cause a fight. When this situation occurs, we have a group meeting, and the whole thing is brought out in the open and de-fused. We have found that the Negro boy here is bigger, stronger, and healthier than the white boy, and the Negro boy has gone further in school. Most of the white kids here are rural and most of the Negro kids are urban. So you have an unsophisticated white boy and a sophisticated Negro boy, who is also physically and mentally further developed. The result is that the Negro kid comes to the forefront in all the activities. All four officers of the House of Representatives are Negro kids, because even the white boys pick out these fellows who seem to be showing aggressive leadership ability. When we call for volunteers for our athletic teams, they end up all Negro. So we're being a little more aggressive with the white kids. We soon realized that just because they were standing on the sidelines didn't mean they wanted to. We're *making* them come out, because we feel they need it. When they get on teams with Negro kids, they

Learning to drive is an important activity at Job Corps centers (OEO)

get along very well. The Negroes want the program to be integrated."

I asked Mr. Kurth if the dropout rate was higher among the white Corpsmen than among the Negroes.

"It's about four times higher for white kids," he replied. "The white dropouts are mainly rural kids from the South. They seem to find it very hard to adjust. Homesickness gets them down, and they just don't have the drive that the Negro kids from the big cities have. Another thing is that most of the Negro kids come from broken homes. They've been kicked around, and they don't have as much to go home to as most of the white Southern kids. Their families are usually intact, and they can go home and settle in. The na-

135

tional dropout rate for the Corps is about twenty-six percent. Here it's about twenty percent. That includes both those who leave voluntarily and those who are dismissed. If a kid refuses to go to class or just to get into the program at all—in other words, if he is a fairly serious offender—we put him in a special group. We call it—it isn't a very good name—the Intensive Treatment Dormitory, and the idea is to try to do something to develop the kid's motivation. The ones who get assigned to this group live together in a special dormitory—No. 2103. Out of two thousand kids, we have fifteen or twenty in there at any given time. We have special counsellors to give them intensive counselling, and we try different methods with their work. For example, we may put them on a partial program—just a half day of classes—or we may give them a whole day of just vocation or a whole day of just academic. We try to find whatever seems right for the individual kid. We figure we have thirty days to get him into the program or face the decision to get him out. We're salvaging about seventy-five percent of these kids. That boy over there leaning back in his chair is an example. He was a very serious problem during his first month here. He wouldn't go to class, he would fight, he would horseplay in the dormitory. He would stay up after hours. He wouldn't help clean up the dorm. He was belligerent toward everybody. His own group voted to put him in 2103. They simply told him he couldn't stay in the dorm, because he was disrupting everything for the thirty-one other people. He came out of 2103 in two weeks. He asked to go back to his old dorm, they voted to take him back, and we haven't had a behavior problem with him since. We're trying not to have any stigma attached to being in 2103. We want it to be considered a special treatment area for kids who have a problem. We don't want to

Putting the finishing touches on a pie at a Job Corps center (OEO)

look on a problem around here as something that's bad." . . .

The lunch period was now nearly over, and Mr. Kurth left to return to his office. Since my plan, as I had told him, was to spend part of the afternoon talking with a few of the Corpsmen and looking in on some of the classes, I stayed behind and moved over to a nearby table, where I struck up a conversation with a couple of Corpsmen who were just finishing second helpings of ice cream. One of them, a Negro boy wearing well-pressed slacks and an expensive-looking sweater, introduced himself as Willie James Greer. He told me that he was twenty-one, came from East St. Louis,

Illinois, and had left school in the eleventh grade. "Quittin' school—that was the biggest mistake I made in my life," he said. (Like all the Corpsmen I talked to, he dropped the "g" in almost every word with an "ing" ending.) "It wasn't that the subjects were too hard or I got behind. Wanting to have my own money —that was most of all my problem. You know, when you're going to school, you like to have money in your pocket and wear fine clothes. You can't hardly do this unless your parents are wealthy, which my parents is not. My father died when I was small. My mother worked as a cook in a café. I have two brothers and two sisters. They're all in school, doing O.K. My main problem was wanting to get the coin. And buying clothes—that was my downfall. When I quit school, I got a job as a janitor, and then I worked for a chemical company. I got approximately eighty dollars take-home. It was nice. I helped my mother pay bills. And I bought some clothes. But I found out that the coin wasn't the only thing, so when I heard about the Job Corps, I went down to see the man. He explained parts of it, and it sounded really good. I went back home and talked to my mother. She said, 'It's your life. You only get one chance in life. When chance come, you better take it.' I thought about this, and I said to myself, 'This is your last chance.' So I'm here. When you first get here, they take you on a tour of the vocational classes, and I decided to go into welding. I'm doing all right. The fellows in the dorm, they're nicer than when I first went in there. At first, you go to bed at night, and when you wake up, your whole face is full of shaving cream. You know, guys horsing around. Now we got our own self-government in our dorm. Made laws. Made rules. I knew this wasn't going to be no paradise, but it's working out O.K. for me."

FURTHER INQUIRY

1. What would prompt Corpsmen to leave? What features might be adopted to encourage them to stay?
2. How can racial feeling in the Job Corps be eliminated?
3. How do you account for the physical and mental superiority of the Negro Job Corpsman as compared with the white?
4. To what extent is Willie's reason for dropping out of school similar to the reasons of some of the dropouts you know?
5. Would you say that the Job Corps is an effective weapon in the "War on Poverty"?

Harvard economist and former United States Ambassador to India, Mr. Galbraith was among the first to point out in his book *The Affluent Society* the existence of hard-core poverty in our otherwise rich American society. Why does Mr. Galbraith put so much emphasis on education as a strategic step in eliminating poverty? Why is education by itself not a cure-all for poverty?

14. The Affluent Society

by JOHN KENNETH GALBRAITH

THE first strategic step in an attack on poverty is to see that it is no longer self-perpetuating. This means insuring that the investment in children from families presently afflicted be as little below normal as possible. If the children of poor families have first-rate schools and school attendance is properly enforced; if the children, though badly fed at home, are well nourished at school; if the community has sound health services, and the physical well-being of

From *The Affluent Society* by John Kenneth Galbraith (Boston: Houghton Mifflin Company, 1958), pp. 323–333. Copyright © 1958 by John Kenneth Galbraith. Reprinted by permission of Houghton Mifflin Company.

the children is vigilantly watched; if there is opportunity for advanced education for those who qualify
regardless of means; and if, especially in the case of
urban communities, law and order are well enforced
and recreation is adequate—then there is a very good
chance that the children of the very poor will come to
maturity without grave disadvantage. In the case of
insular poverty* this remedy requires that the services of the community be assisted from outside.
Poverty is self-perpetuating because the poorest communities are poorest in the services which would eliminate it. To eliminate poverty efficiently we should
invest more than proportionately in the children of the
poor community. It is there that high quality schools,
strong health services, special provision for nutrition
and recreation are most needed to compensate for the
very low investment which families are able to make
in their own offspring.

The effect of education and related investment in
individuals is to enable them either to contend more
effectively with their environment, or to escape it and
take up life elsewhere on more or less equal terms
with others. The role of education as an antidote* to
the homing instinct which crowds people into the areas
of inadequate opportunity and frustration is also
clear. However, in the strategy of the attack on insular poverty a place remains for an attack on the
frustrations of environment itself. This is particularly
clear in the case of the slum. Slum clearance and
expansion of low and middle income housing removes

---

insular poverty—islands of poverty, as in ghetto slums or
  rural sections where all people are poor and stay that
  way.

antidote—opposite force.

Investing in good schools for the children of the poor is one of the best ways to insure that the next generation will become employable citizens, able to break the cycle of poverty (OEO)

142

a comprehensive set* of frustrations and greatly widens opportunity.

Nor is case poverty in the contemporary generation wholly intransigent.* Much can be done to treat those characteristics which cause people to reject or be rejected by the modern industrial society. Educational deficiencies can be overcome. Mental deficiencies can be treated. Physical handicaps can be remedied. The limiting factor is not knowledge of what can be done. Overwhelmingly it is our failure to invest in people.

FURTHER INQUIRY

1. Why should we invest more than proportionately in the children of the poor community?
2. Do you think that better housing can help to end poverty?
3. Would you say that Galbraith is optimistic about what can be done? On what grounds would you agree or disagree with his suggestions?

---

comprehensive set—group.

intransigent—beyond remedy.

In this brief article, Martin Luther King touches on a very complex issue. He suggests, as have others, that the only way to solve poverty is to assure all a minimum yearly income. Consider: Is it fair to provide the poor with a minimum income when they are not working?

15. Abolish Poverty Directly

by MARTIN LUTHER KING, JR.

I am now convinced that the simplest approach to solving the problem of poverty will prove to be the most effective. The solution is to abolish it directly by the guaranteed income.*

Two conditions are indispensable if we are to insure that the guaranteed income operates as a consistently

---

guaranteed income—assured payments of money.

From *Where Do We Go From Here: Chaos or Community?* by Martin Luther King, Jr. (New York: Harper & Row, Publishers, 1967), pp. 162–166. Copyright © 1967 by Martin Luther King, Jr. Originally appeared in *The New York Times Magazine*, under the title "Abolish Poverty Directly." Reprinted by permission of Harper & Row, Publishers.

Project Head Start gives four- and five-year-olds from culturally deprived homes the tools they will need to start school on the same level as more fortunate children (UPI)

progressive measure. First, it must be pegged to the median* income of society, not at the lowest levels of income. To guarantee an income at the floor would simply perpetuate welfare standards and freeze into the society poverty conditions.

Second, it must automatically increase as the total social income grows. Were it permitted to remain static under growth conditions, the recipients would suffer a relative decline. Without these safeguards a creeping retrogression* would occur nullifying* the gains of security and stability.

---

median—mid-point between the highest and lowest.

retrogression—falling back.

nullifying—doing away with; ending.

Three fruits are offered to the poor here—a federal welfare system with nationwide standards, job training, and the guaranteed minimum income.—James Flora. Reprinted by permission of *The New York Times*.

This is not a "civil rights" program in the sense that that term is currently used. The program would benefit all the poor, including the two-thirds of them who are white. I hope that both Negro and white will act in coalition* to effect this change, because their combined strength will be necessary to overcome the fierce opposition we must realistically anticipate.

Our nation's adjustment to a new mode of thinking will be facilitated if we realize that for nearly 40 years two groups in our society have already been enjoying a guaranteed income: the wealthy who own securities have always had an assured income; and their polar opposite, the relief clients, have been guaranteed an income, however minuscule, through welfare benefits.

The curse of poverty has no justification in our age. It is socially as cruel and blind as the practice of cannibalism at the dawn of civilization, when men ate each other because they had not yet learned to take food from the soil or to consume the abundant animal life around them. The time has come for us to civilize ourselves by the total, direct and immediate abolition of poverty.

---

in coalition—together.

FURTHER INQUIRY

1. To what extent is a minimum income for all likely to contribute to an end to poverty? About how much should that figure be? How did you decide on it?
2. Comment on the comparison King makes between modern poverty and primitive cannibalism.
3. Is it reasonable to peg a guaranteed income to the middle income rather than to the lowest? Why or why not?
4. What relationship may be said to exist between civil rights and the problem of poverty?

Notes

**Suggestions for
Additional Reading**

Index

Notes

1. Michael Harrington, *The Other America* (New York: Penguin Books paperback edition, 1964), Chapter I, p. 9.
2. Charles Abrams, "Rich Country, Poor Cities," *The New York Times Book Review,* July 16, 1967, p. 21.
3. Sargent Shriver, "Interview with Sargent Shriver," *U.S. News and World Report,* February 28, 1966, pp. 64–69.
4. Lee Dirks, "Poverty Is a Simple Issue," *The National Observer,* January 27, 1964, Vol. 3, No. 4, p. 1.
5. Lee Dirks, *Ibid.,* p. 1.
6. Robert Hunter, *Poverty* (New York: Harper Torchbooks paperback edition, 1964), p. 52.
7. Lee Dirks, *Ibid.,* p. 1.
8. "Everyone Is Discovering Poverty in America," *The International Teamster Magazine,* February, 1964, p. 16.
9. John Kenneth Galbraith, *The Affluent Society* (New York: Mentor Books, New American Library, 1958), pp. 252–253.

10. Burton A. Weisbrod, ed., *The Economics of Poverty* (Englewood Cliffs, N.J.: Prentice-Hall, 1965), p. 191.

11. *Report of the President,* Appalachia Regional Commission, 1964, p. 131.

12. Charles Abrams, *The City Is the Frontier* (New York: Harper & Row, Publishers, 1965), p. 96.

13. Andrew Carnegie, *The Gospel of Wealth.* Quoted in Robert E. Will and Harold G. Vetter, eds., *Poverty in Affluence* (New York: Harcourt, Brace and World, Inc., 1965), p. 65.

14. Robert H. Bremner, *From the Depths* (New York: New York University Press, 1964), p. 7.

15. *Ibid.,* p. 47.

16. *Ibid.,* p. 51.

Suggestions for Additional Reading

1. ABRAMS, CHARLES, *The City Is the Frontier*. New York: Harper & Row, Publishers, 1965. This noted housing authority writes about the work that must yet be done if the people of the city are to live in harmony and comfort.
2. BREMNER, ROBERT H., *From the Depths*. New York: New York University Press, 1964. This volume traces the attitudes of Americans toward poverty and the poor.
3. ELMAN, RICHARD G., *The Poorhouse State*. New York: Pantheon Books, 1966. This volume describes the ineffective efforts that have been made to help the poor.
4. MAY, EDGAR, *The Wasted Americans*. New York: Harper & Row, Publishers, 1964. The author takes a critical look at the cost of welfare and the waste of human resources resulting from poverty.
5. MILLER, HERMAN P., *Rich Man, Poor Man*. New York: Thomas Y. Crowell Company, 1964. This volume provides a study in contrasts between the income and life styles of the well-to-do and those of the poor.

153

6. STEWARD, MAXWELL, *The Poor Among Us—Challenge and Opportunity.* New York: Public Affairs Pamphlet Company, 1967. A brief but well-organized and well-presented discussion of poverty in the United States is presented here.

Index

GENERAL EDITOR

Gerald Leinwand is Professor of Education and Chairman of the Department of Education at the Bernard M. Baruch College of the City University of New York. Dr. Leinwand received his B.A., M.S., and Ph.D degrees from New York University and an M.A. from Columbia University. In addition to numerous magazine articles, he is the author of *The Pageant of World History, The American Constitution: A Tutor-Text,* and a college text *Teaching History and the Social Studies in Secondary Schools.*

The Diary of the American Revolution

Compiled by Frank Moore

Edited, Abridged, and with an Introduction
by John Anthony Scott

A rare collection of reports and opinion from British, Tory and Revolutionary sources, 1775 to 1781

"A thoroughly enlightening and entertaining edition ... the selections from colonial newspapers—on-the-spot stories, political essays, diatribes, humorous features—are wonderfully vivid reading."

—*Publishers' Weekly*

Illustrated with eight steel engravings, ten facsimile broadsides, and augmented with ballads and songs.

Hardcover   19645 $7.95   *Paperback   48403 $1.45*

Living Documents in American History

Edited and with Introductions by John Anthony Scott

Two rich and provocative collections of original documents—letters, essays, sermons, manifestos, speeches, court cases, and songs—tracing the struggle for interracial democracy in the United State

Volume I

From Earliest Colonial Times to the Civil War

Including: An Account of the Slave Trade / The Massachusetts Body of Liberties / The Lincoln-Douglas Debates / as well as numerous documents of The Great Awakening, and America's surge westward.

Hardcover   98088 $5.95   *Paperback   W•1040   90¢*

Volume II

From Reconstruction to the Outbreak of World War I

Including: The Radical, Moderate and Conservative positions on Reconstruction / Andrew Carnegie on Wealth / The Civil Rights Cases of 1883 / as well as major contributions from The Gilded Age, America's rise as a world power, and the Progressive Era.

Hardcover   42699 $7.95

WSP
ⓃWASHINGTON SQUARE PRESS

If your bookseller does not have these titles you may order them by sending retail price, plus 15¢ per book for mailing and handling to MAIL SERVICE DEPARTMENT, Washington Square Press, a division of Simon & Schuster, Inc., 1 West 39th St., New York, N.Y. 10018. Please send check or money order—do not send cash.   W 19/9